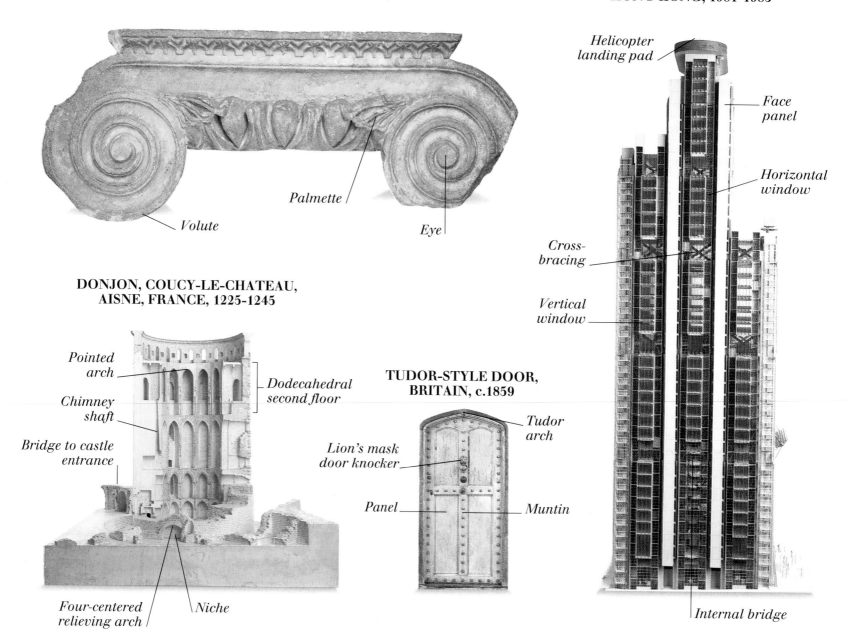

IONIC CAPITAL, THE PROPYLAEUM (GATEWAY), TEMPLE OF ATHENA POLIAS, PRIENE, GREECE, c.334 BC

Volute

Palmette

Eye

HONG KONG AND SHANGHAI BANK, HONG KONG, 1981-1985

Helicopter landing pad

Face panel

Horizontal window

Cross-bracing

Vertical window

Internal bridge

DONJON, COUCY-LE-CHATEAU, AISNE, FRANCE, 1225-1245

Pointed arch

Chimney shaft

Bridge to castle entrance

Dodecahedral second floor

Four-centered relieving arch

Niche

TUDOR-STYLE DOOR, BRITAIN, c.1859

Tudor arch

Lion's mask door knocker

Panel

Muntin

CRYSTAL PALACE EXHIBITION HALL, LONDON, BRITAIN, 1851

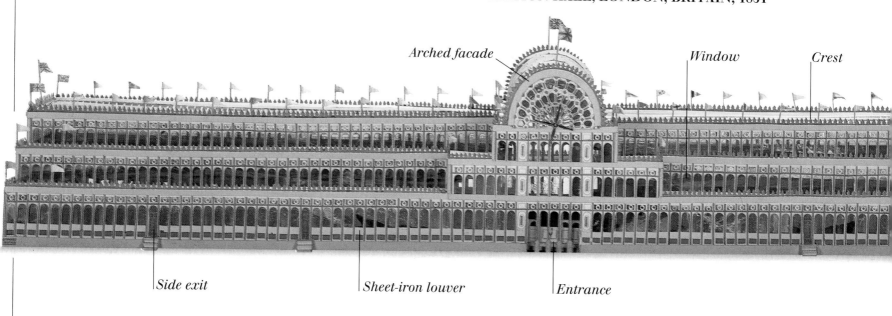

Arched facade

Window

Crest

Side exit

Sheet-iron louver

Entrance

EYEWITNESS VISUAL DICTIONARIES

THE VISUAL
DICTIONARY *of*
BUILDINGS

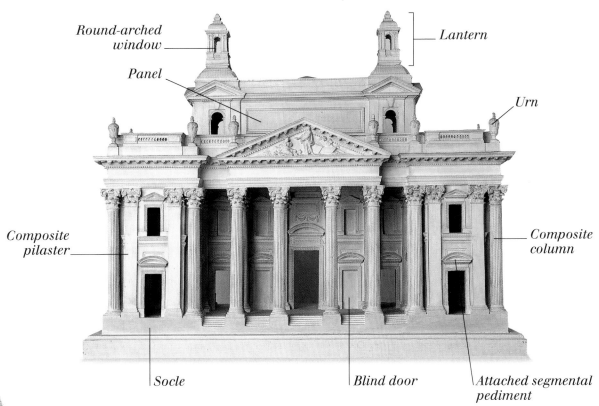

Round-arched window

Panel

Lantern

Urn

Composite pilaster

Composite column

Socle

Blind door

Attached segmental pediment

PROPOSED FACADE, THE MADELEINE, PARIS, FRANCE, 1764

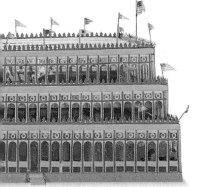

Stoddart

A DORLING KINDERSLEY BOOK

PROJECT ART EDITOR NICOLA LIDDIARD
DESIGNER PAUL CALVER

PROJECT EDITOR ROGER TRITTON
EDITOR FIONA COURTENAY-THOMPSON
CONSULTANT EDITOR ALEXANDRA KENNEDY
U.S. EDITOR CHARLES A. WILLS

MANAGING ART EDITOR STEPHEN KNOWLDEN
SENIOR EDITOR MARTYN PAGE
MANAGING EDITOR RUTH MIDGLEY

PHOTOGRAPHY TIM RIDLEY, ANDY CRAWFORD
ILLUSTRATIONS JOHN WOODCOCK, SIMONE END, KATHLEEN MCDOUGALL

PRODUCTION HILARY STEPHENS

Corinthian capital
Naos (cella) window
Drum
Cornice
Podium

TEMPLE OF VESTA, TIVOLI, ITALY, c.80 BC

FIRST PUBLISHED IN CANADA IN 1992 BY STODDART PUBLISHING CO. LIMITED
34 LESMILL ROAD, TORONTO, CANADA, M3B 2T6

PUBLISHED IN GREAT BRITAIN IN 1992
BY DORLING KINDERSLEY LIMITED, 9 HENRIETTA STREET, COVENT GARDEN, LONDON WC2E 8PS, ENGLAND

COPYRIGHT © 1992 DORLING KINDERSLEY LIMITED, LONDON

CANADIAN CATALOGUING IN PUBLICATION DATA
MAIN ENTRY UNDER TITLE:
THE VISUAL DICTIONARY OF BUILDINGS
(EYEWITNESS VISUAL DICTIONARIES)

ISBN 0-7737-2635-7

1. ARCHITECTURE - PICTORIAL WORKS - JUVENILE LITERATURE.
2. ARCHITECTURE - TERMINOLOGY - JUVENILE LITERATURE. 3. DECORATION AND ORNAMENT,
ARCHITECTURAL - PICTORIAL WORKS - JUVENILE LITERATURE. 4. DECORATION AND ORNAMENT,
ARCHITECTURAL - TERMINOLOGY - JUVENILE LITERATURE. 5. BUILDINGS - TERMINOLOGY -
JUVENILE LITERATURE. 6. PICTURE DICTIONARIES, ENGLISH - JUVENILE LITERATURE.
I. SERIES.

NA31.V578 1992 j720'.3 C92-093940-6

REPRODUCED BY COLOURSCAN, SINGAPORE
PRINTED AND BOUND BY ARNOLDO MONDADORI, VERONA, ITALY

Contents

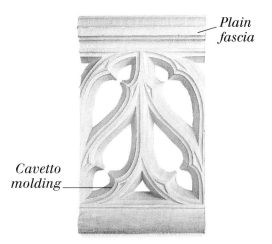

Palm leaf

Lotus stem

Lotus bud

PLANT CAPITAL OF THE PTOLEMAIC-ROMAN PERIOD, EGYPT, 332-30 BC

ANCIENT EGYPT 6

ANCIENT GREECE 8

ANCIENT ROME 10

WALLS 14

ROOFS AND CHIMNEYS 16

MEDIEVAL CASTLES AND HOUSES 18

MEDIEVAL CHURCHES 20

GOTHIC 22

RENAISSANCE 26

BAROQUE AND NEOCLASSICAL 30

CEILINGS 36

ARCHES AND VAULTS 38

DOMES 40

ISLAMIC BUILDINGS 42

SOUTH AND EAST ASIA 44

DOORS 46

WINDOWS 48

THE 19TH CENTURY 50

THE EARLY 20TH CENTURY 52

MODERN BUILDINGS 54

ARCHITECTURAL STYLES 58

INDEX 60

ACKNOWLEDGMENTS 64

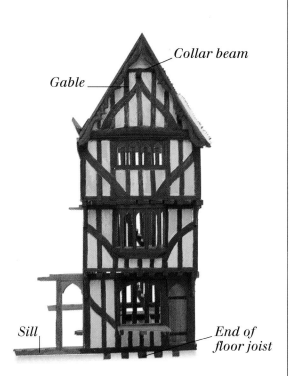

Plain fascia

Cavetto molding

GOTHIC CURVILINEAR (FLOWING) TRACERY

Circular molding

VICTORIAN MOLDED BRICK

Arris

"RUBBER" (SOFT, EASILY-SPLIT) BRICK

Round arch

Architrave

Socle

Barley-sugar column

ROUND ARCH AND BARLEY-SUGAR COLUMNS

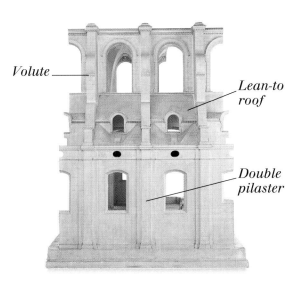

Volute

Lean-to roof

Double pilaster

CHURCH OF ST. PAUL-ST. LOUIS, PARIS, FRANCE, FROM 1627

Collar beam

Gable

Sill

End of floor joist

TIMBER-FRAMED HOUSE, BRITAIN, c.1450

Ancient Egypt

THE CIVILIZATION OF THE ANCIENT EGYPTIANS (which lasted from about 3100 BC until it was finally absorbed into the Roman empire in 30 BC) is famous for its temples and tombs. Egyptian temples were often huge and geometric, like the Temple of Amon-Re (below and right). They were usually decorated with hieroglyphs (sacred characters used for picture writing) and painted reliefs depicting gods, Pharaohs (kings), and queens. Tombs were particularly important to the Egyptians, who believed that the dead were resurrected in the afterlife. The tombs were often decorated—as, for example, the surround of the false door opposite— in order to give comfort to the dead. The best-known ancient Egyptian tombs are the pyramids (see pp. 58-59), which were designed to symbolize the rays of the sun. Many of the architectural forms used by the ancient Egyptians were later adopted by other civilizations. For example, columns and capitals were later used by the ancient Greeks (see pp. 8-9) and ancient Romans (see pp. 10-11).

SIDE VIEW OF HYPOSTYLE HALL, TEMPLE OF AMON-RE, KARNAK, EGYPT, c.1290 BC

FRONT VIEW OF HYPOSTYLE HALL, TEMPLE OF AMON-RE

Cornice decorated with cavetto molding

Campaniform (open papyrus) capital

Architrave

Papyrus-bud capital

Socle

Side aisle   Central nave   Side aisle

Horus, the sun-god   Architrave   Stone slab forming flat roof of side aisle

Kepresh crown with disc

Chons, the moon-god   Amon-Re, king of the gods   Hathor, the sky-goddess   Papyrus motif   Cartouche (oval border) containing the titles of the Pharaoh (king)   Socle   Aisle running north–south

LIMESTONE FALSE DOOR WITH HIEROGLYPHS, TOMB OF KING TJETJI, GIZA, EGYPT, c.2400 BC

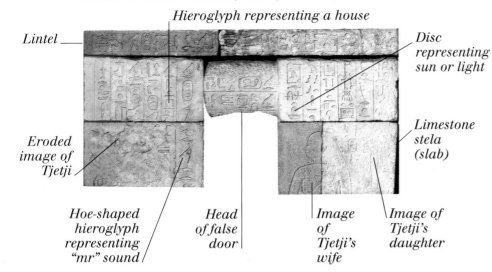

Lintel

Hieroglyph representing a house

Disc representing sun or light

Eroded image of Tjetji

Limestone stela (slab)

Hoe-shaped hieroglyph representing "mr" sound

Head of false door

Image of Tjetji's wife

Image of Tjetji's daughter

PLANT CAPITAL OF THE PTOLEMAIC-ROMAN PERIOD, EGYPT, 332-30 BC

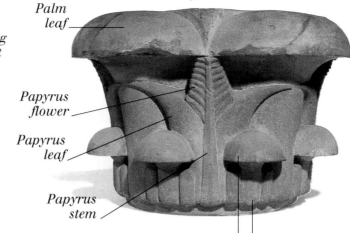

Palm leaf

Papyrus flower

Papyrus leaf

Papyrus stem

Lotus bud

Lotus stem

Cornice decorated with cavetto molding

Bead molding

Trellis window

Rectangular pier decorated with hieroglyphs

Elevated roof of central nave

Clerestory

Disc representing sun or light

Architrave

Square abacus

Papyrus-bud capital

Papyriform column

Shaft

Scene depicting a Pharaoh (king) paying homage to the god Amon-Re

Central nave

ANCIENT EGYPTIAN BUILDING DECORATION

DECORATED WINDOW, MEDINET HABU, EGYPT, c.1198 BC

ROPE AND PATERAE DECORATION

CAPITAL WITH THE HEAD OF THE SKY-GODDESS HATHOR, TEMPLE OF ISIS, PHILAE, EGYPT, 283-47 BC

LOTUS AND PAPYRUS FRIEZE DECORATION

Ancient Greece

THE CLASSICAL TEMPLES OF ANCIENT GREECE were built according to the belief that certain forms and proportions were pleasing to the gods. There were three main Ancient Greek architectural orders (styles), which can be distinguished by the decoration and proportions of their columns, capitals (column tops), and entablatures (structures resting on the capitals). The oldest is the Doric order, which dates from the seventh century BC and was used mainly on the Greek mainland and in the western colonies, such as Sicily and southern Italy. The Temple of Neptune, shown here, is a classic example of this order. It is hypaethral (roofless) and peripteral (surrounded by a single row of columns). About a century later, the more decorative Ionic order developed on the Aegean Islands. Features of this order include volutes (spiral scrolls) on capitals and acroteria (pediment ornaments). The Corinthian order was invented in Athens in the fifth century BC and is typically identified by an acanthus leaf on the capitals. This order was later widely used in ancient Roman architecture.

CAPITALS OF THE THREE ORDERS OF ANCIENT GREEK ARCHITECTURE

- Abacus
- Echinus
- Trachelion (neck)
- Annulet

DORIC CAPITAL, THE PROPYLAEUM (GATEWAY), THE ACROPOLIS, ATHENS, GREECE, 449 BC

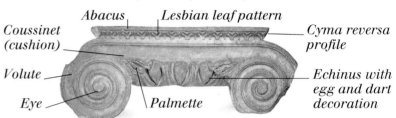

- Coussinet (cushion)
- Abacus
- Lesbian leaf pattern
- Cyma reversa profile
- Volute
- Echinus with egg and dart decoration
- Eye
- Palmette

IONIC CAPITAL, THE PROPYLAEUM (GATEWAY), TEMPLE OF ATHENA POLIAS, PRIENE, GREECE, c.334 BC

- Mask
- Abacus
- Volute
- Cauliculus
- Acanthus leaf
- Bell-shaped core

CORINTHIAN CAPITAL FROM A STOA (PORTICO), PROBABLY FROM ASIA MINOR

TEMPLE OF NEPTUNE, PAESTUM, ITALY, c.460 BC

- Raking cornice
- Pediment
- Trachelion (neck)
- Taenia
- Triglyph
- Metope
- Glyph (channel)
- Doric entablature
- Pteron (external colonnade)
- Euthynteria
- Drum
- Stylobate
- Column of the Doric order

PLAN OF THE TEMPLE OF NEPTUNE, PAESTUM

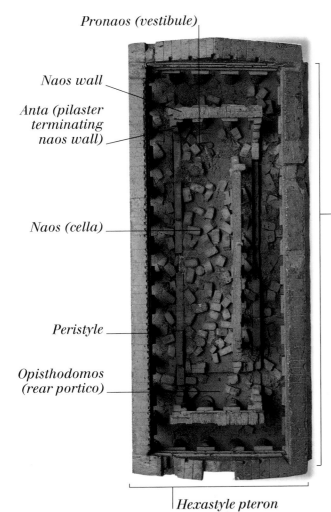

Pronaos (vestibule)

Naos wall

Anta (pilaster terminating naos wall)

Naos (cella)

Pteron (external colonnade)

Peristyle

Opisthodomos (rear portico)

Hexastyle pteron (colonnade of six columns)

ANCIENT GREEK BUILDING DECORATION

Volute

FACADE, TREASURY OF ATREUS, MYCENAE, GREECE, 1350-1250 BC

Meander

FRETWORK, PARTHENON, ATHENS, GREECE, 447-436 BC

ACROTERION, TEMPLE OF APHAIA, AEGINA, GREECE, 490 BC

Griffon (gryphon)

Raking cornice

ANTEFIXA, TEMPLE OF APHAIA, AEGINA, GREECE, 490 BC

Palmette

Volute

Regula (short fillet beneath taenia)

Eaves

Cornice

Frieze

Architrave

Capital

Shaft

Crepidoma (stepped base)

Entasis (slight curve of a column)

Intercolumniation

Fluting

Ancient Rome 1

IN THE EARLY PERIOD OF THE ROMAN EMPIRE extensive use was made of ancient Greek architectural ideas, particularly those of the Corinthian order (see pp. 8-9). As a result, many early Roman buildings—such as the Temple of Vesta (opposite)—closely resemble ancient Greek buildings. A distinctive Roman style began to evolve in the first century AD. This style developed the interiors of buildings (the Greeks had concentrated on the exterior) by wing arches, vaults, and domes inside the buildings and by ornamenting internal walls; many of these features can be seen in the Pantheon. Exterior columns were often used for decorative rather than structural purposes, as in the Colosseum and the Porta Nigra (see pp. 12-13). Smaller buildings had timber frames with wattle-and-daub walls, as in the mill (see pp. 12-13). Roman architecture remained influential for many centuries, with some of its principles being used in the 11th century in Romanesque buildings (see pp. 20-21) and also in the 15th and 16th centuries in Renaissance buildings (see pp. 26-29).

ANCIENT ROMAN BUILDING DECORATION

FESTOON, TEMPLE OF VESTA,
TIVOLI, ITALY, c.80 BC

RICHLY DECORATED
ROMAN OVUM

INTERIOR OF THE PANTHEON, ROME, ITALY, 118-c.128

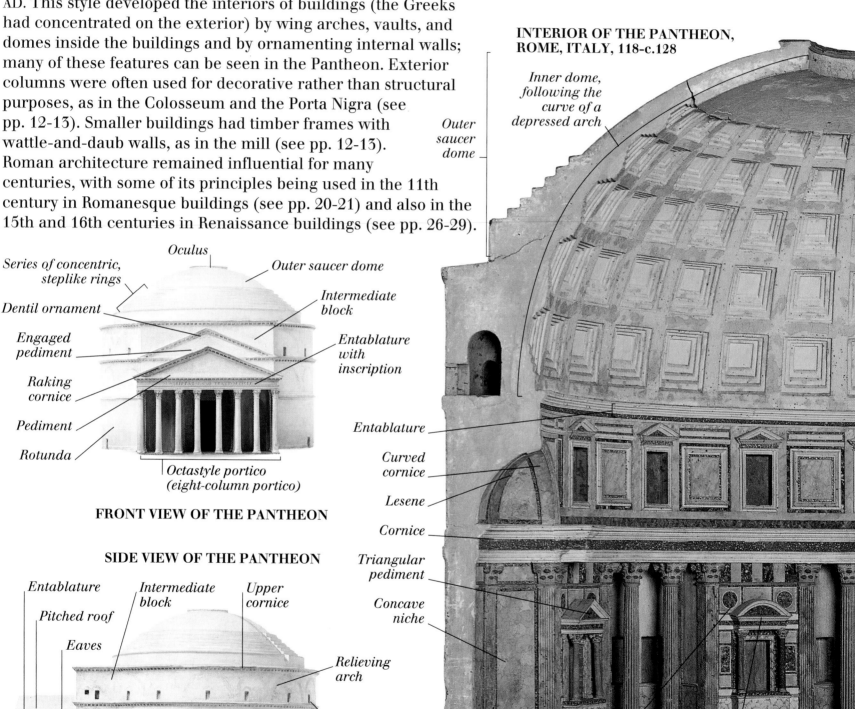

Inner dome, following the curve of a depressed arch

Outer saucer dome

Entablature

Curved cornice

Lesene

Cornice

Triangular pediment

Concave niche

Marble veneer   Segmental pediment   Pedestal

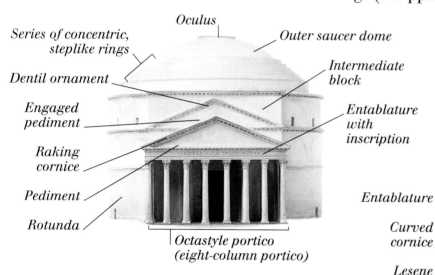

Series of concentric, steplike rings

Oculus

Outer saucer dome

Dentil ornament

Intermediate block

Engaged pediment

Entablature with inscription

Raking cornice

Pediment

Rotunda

Octastyle portico (eight-column portico)

FRONT VIEW OF THE PANTHEON

SIDE VIEW OF THE PANTHEON

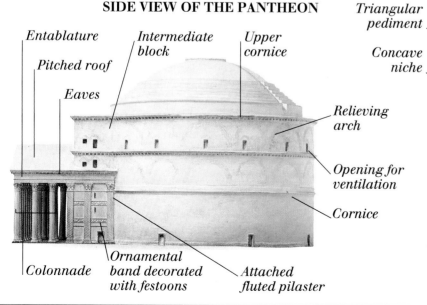

Entablature

Intermediate block

Upper cornice

Pitched roof

Eaves

Relieving arch

Opening for ventilation

Cornice

Colonnade

Ornamental band decorated with festoons

Attached fluted pilaster

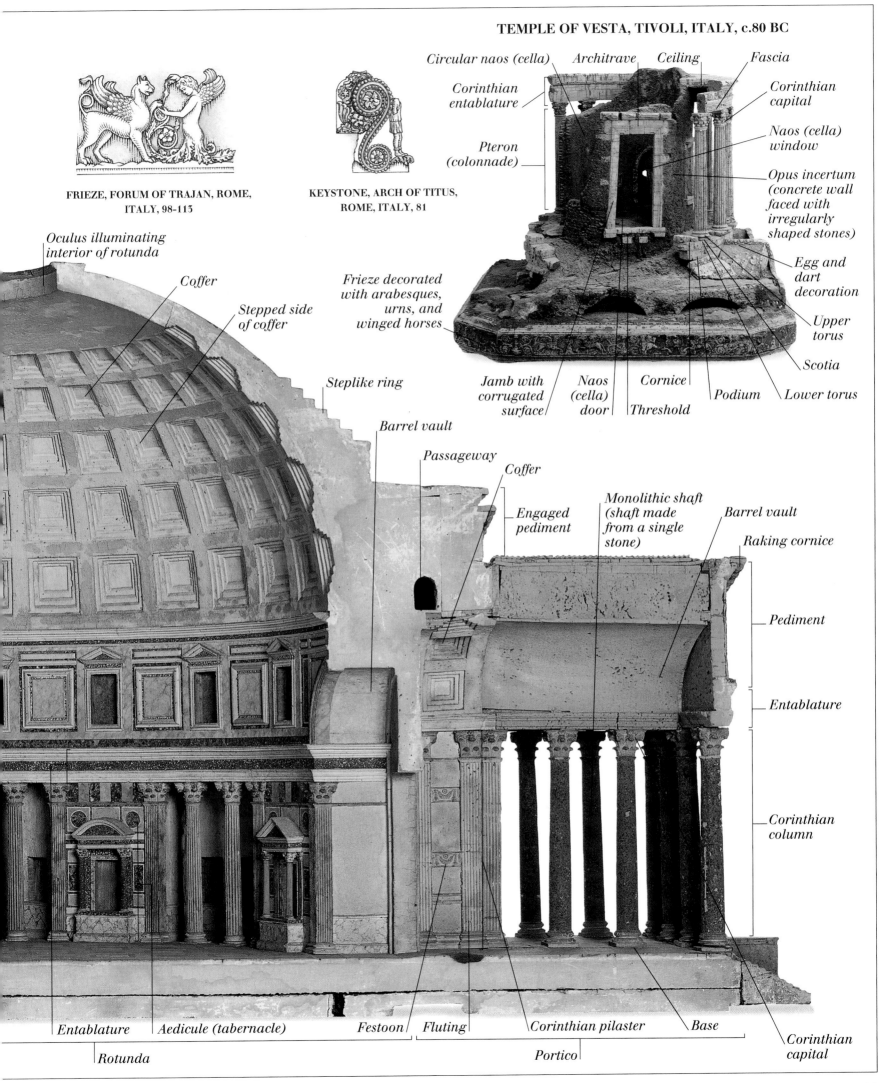

FRIEZE, FORUM OF TRAJAN, ROME, ITALY, 98-113

KEYSTONE, ARCH OF TITUS, ROME, ITALY, 81

TEMPLE OF VESTA, TIVOLI, ITALY, c.80 BC

Circular naos (cella)

Architrave

Ceiling

Fascia

Corinthian entablature

Corinthian capital

Naos (cella) window

Pteron (colonnade)

Opus incertum (concrete wall faced with irregularly shaped stones)

Egg and dart decoration

Upper torus

Scotia

Lower torus

Jamb with corrugated surface

Naos (cella) door

Cornice

Threshold

Podium

Oculus illuminating interior of rotunda

Coffer

Stepped side of coffer

Frieze decorated with arabesques, urns, and winged horses

Steplike ring

Barrel vault

Passageway

Coffer

Engaged pediment

Monolithic shaft (shaft made from a single stone)

Barrel vault

Raking cornice

Pediment

Entablature

Corinthian column

Entablature

Aedicule (tabernacle)

Festoon

Fluting

Corinthian pilaster

Base

Corinthian capital

Rotunda

Portico

Ancient Rome 2

SIDE VIEW OF A ROMAN MILL

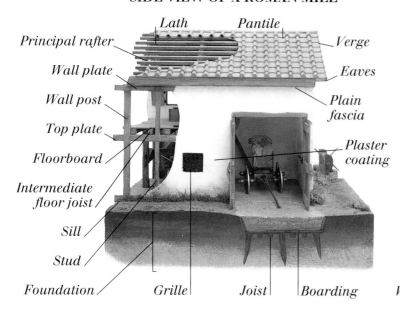

Principal rafter
Lath
Pantile
Verge
Wall plate
Eaves
Wall post
Plain fascia
Top plate
Plaster coating
Floorboard
Intermediate floor joist
Sill
Stud
Foundation
Grille
Joist
Boarding

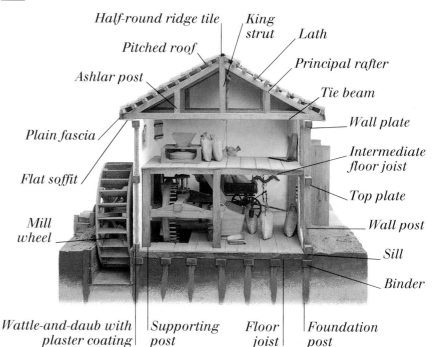

Half-round ridge tile
King strut
Lath
Pitched roof
Principal rafter
Ashlar post
Tie beam
Plain fascia
Wall plate
Intermediate floor joist
Flat soffit
Top plate
Mill wheel
Wall post
Sill
Binder
Wattle-and-daub with plaster coating
Supporting post
Floor joist
Foundation post

THE COLOSSEUM (FLAVIAN AMPHITHEATER), ROME, ITALY, 70-82

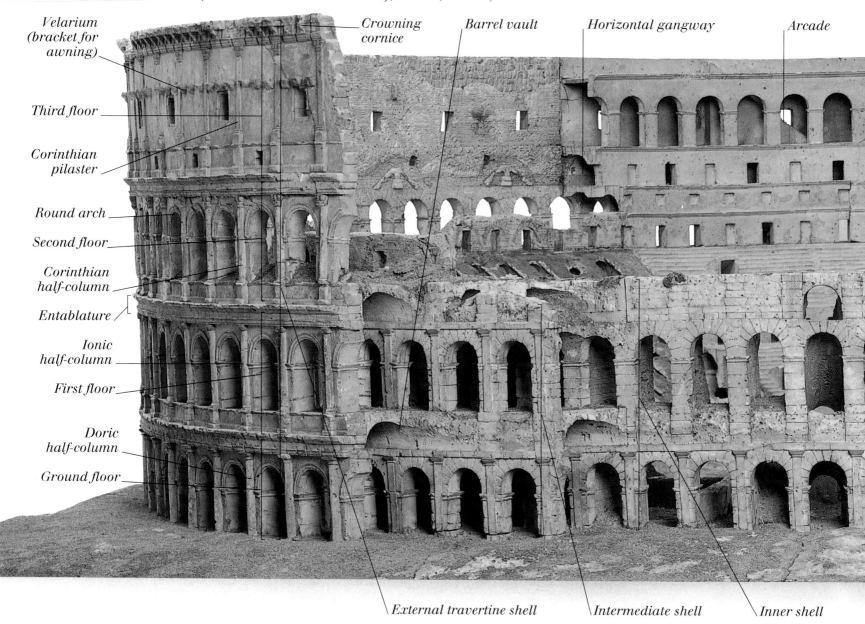

Velarium (bracket for awning)
Crowning cornice
Barrel vault
Horizontal gangway
Arcade
Third floor
Corinthian pilaster
Round arch
Second floor
Corinthian half-column
Entablature
Ionic half-column
First floor
Doric half-column
Ground floor
External travertine shell
Intermediate shell
Inner shell

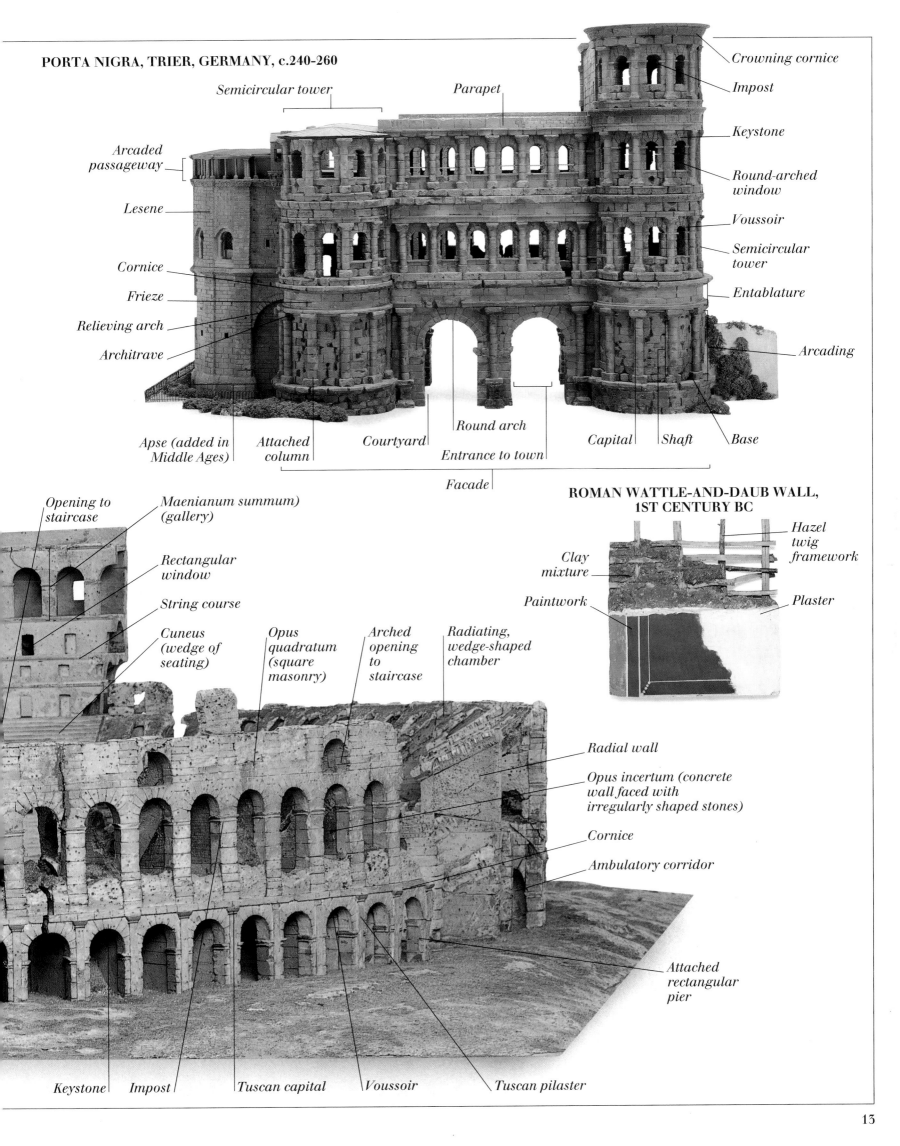

PORTA NIGRA, TRIER, GERMANY, c.240-260

Crowning cornice

Impost

Semicircular tower

Parapet

Keystone

Arcaded passageway

Round-arched window

Lesene

Voussoir

Semicircular tower

Cornice

Entablature

Frieze

Relieving arch

Arcading

Architrave

Apse (added in Middle Ages)

Attached column

Courtyard

Round arch

Entrance to town

Capital

Shaft

Base

Facade

ROMAN WATTLE-AND-DAUB WALL, 1ST CENTURY BC

Opening to staircase

Maenianum summum) (gallery)

Hazel twig framework

Clay mixture

Rectangular window

String course

Paintwork

Plaster

Cuneus (wedge of seating)

Opus quadratum (square masonry)

Arched opening to staircase

Radiating, wedge-shaped chamber

Radial wall

Opus incertum (concrete wall faced with irregularly shaped stones)

Cornice

Ambulatory corridor

Attached rectangular pier

Keystone

Impost

Tuscan capital

Voussoir

Tuscan pilaster

Walls

MEDIEVAL WOODEN WALL ORNAMENT, BRITAIN

A WALL IS A CONTINUOUS structure that encloses or subdivides a building. The two main types of load-bearing outer wall are frame-construction walls and mass-construction walls. Frame-construction walls have a frame of timber or metal. In timber-framed houses, such as the medieval house below, the open panels between the studs (vertical wall timbers) were filled with wattle (thin wooden laths) and daub (mud or clay). The finished house was often embellished with decorative braces and wooden carvings. A mass-construction wall is a solid structure made of brick or stone. Various types of bonding have been developed to increase the strength of brick walls. In English bond, bricks are laid so that alternate courses (layers) on the face of the wall are composed exclusively of either headers (bricks laid widthways) or stretchers (bricks laid lengthways). In Flemish bond, the face of each course consists of alternate headers and stretchers. Stretcher bond is composed of stretchers only. The walls of large buildings were usually built from stone. For example, in St. Paul's Cathedral (opposite), piers (solid masonry supports) bear the weight of huge arches and windows. These piers are decorated with columns and pilasters.

WATTLE AND DAUB

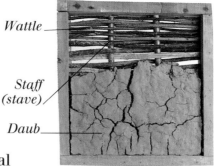

Wattle
Staff (stave)
Daub

BRICKLAYING FORMATIONS

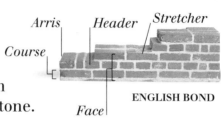

Arris
Header
Stretcher
Course
Face
ENGLISH BOND

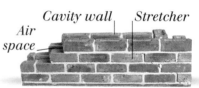

Bed joint
Perpend
Closer
Header
Stretcher
FLEMISH BOND

Cavity wall
Stretcher
Air space
STRETCHER BOND

TYPES OF BRICK

SANDSTONE BRICK

FLINT FACING BRICK

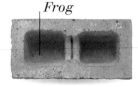

MASS-PRODUCED BRICK, BRITAIN, 19TH CENTURY

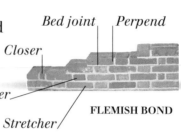

Frog

EARLY METRIC BRICK, BRITAIN, 19TH CENTURY

MODERN ENGINEERING BRICK

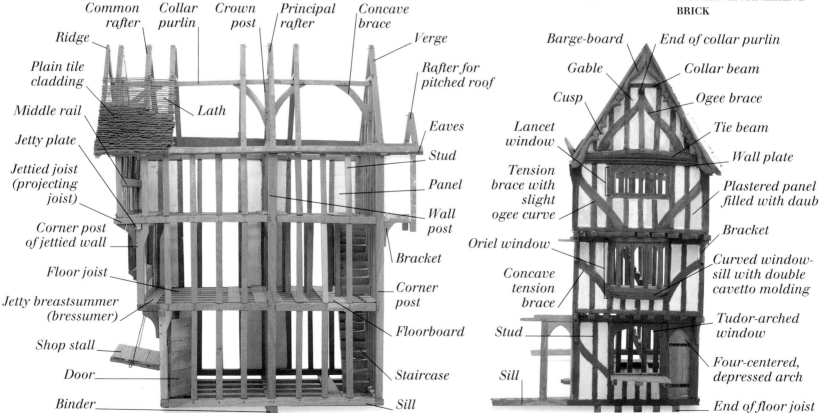

Common rafter
Collar purlin
Crown post
Principal rafter
Concave brace
Ridge
Verge
Plain tile cladding
Rafter for pitched roof
Middle rail
Lath
Eaves
Jetty plate
Stud
Jettied joist (projecting joist)
Panel
Corner post of jettied wall
Wall post
Floor joist
Bracket
Jetty breastsummer (bressumer)
Corner post
Shop stall
Floorboard
Door
Staircase
Binder
Sill

SIDE VIEW OF A TIMBER-FRAMED HOUSE, BRITAIN, c.1450

Barge-board
End of collar purlin
Gable
Collar beam
Cusp
Ogee brace
Lancet window
Tie beam
Tension brace with slight ogee curve
Wall plate
Plastered panel filled with daub
Oriel window
Bracket
Concave tension brace
Curved window-sill with double cavetto molding
Stud
Tudor-arched window
Sill
Four-centered, depressed arch
End of floor joist

FRONT VIEW OF A TIMBER-FRAMED HOUSE

WOODEN RECONSTRUCTION OF A PIER, ST. PAUL'S CATHEDRAL, LONDON, BRITAIN, 1675-1710 (BY C. WREN)

Buttress

Air duct

Pedestal of outer dome

Corridor from inner dome to clerestory

Inner dome

Apex of relieving arch

Clerestory window

Exterior transept wall

Round arch

Semidome

Side-aisle vault

Round, transverse, side-aisle arch

Frieze with carvings of festoons

Composite pilaster

Side aisle

Base

Socle

Cornice

Saucer dome

Pendentive

Arch cutting into main vault

Main vault

Springing point of vault

Attached abutment pier

Cornice

Entablature

Coffered arch

Plain frieze

Cornice

Fascia

Composite capital

Paneling

Paneling

Main vessel

Floor level

Foundation (part of crypt)

VIEW FROM THE NAVE

Inner dome

Inner dome

Relieving arch

"Whispering Gallery"

Molded bracket

Buttress

Passageway

Pedestal of outer dome

Cornice

Triangular buttress

Passageway along upper clerestory wall

Mullioned window

Semidome

Barrel vault

Cornice

Semidome

Barrel vault

Corinthian capital

Coffered arch

Entablature

Composite capital

Frieze

Composite pilaster

Paneling

Base

Socle

Floor level

Segmental arch

Clerestory window

Exterior wall of main elevation

Side-aisle vault

Round arch over passageway

Round-arched hollow

Lunette

Festoon

Wreath carving

Concave, round-arched niche

VIEW FROM A SIDE AISLE

15

Roofs and chimneys

A ROOF HAS TWO BASIC COMPONENTS: a covering and a supporting frame. In pitched (sloping) roofs, the frame consists of inclined rafters and horizontal purlins (timbers) connected to a roof truss by joints such as the mortise and tenon joint or the edge-halfed scarf joint. The most common roof coverings are slates, clay tiles, and asphalt (used to waterproof flat roofs), although thatch and lead are still used, mainly to roof old buildings. A thatched roof consists of layered bundles of straw or reeds attached to the roof with steel or hazel rods and fixed in place by crooks (hooks) driven into the rafters. A chimney consists of a passage (or flue) for the escape of fumes from a fireplace; a chimney stack, which projects above the roof; and a chimney pot on top of the stack. Chimney pots and chimney stacks sometimes have elaborate designs, some of which are shown opposite.

ROOF FINIAL

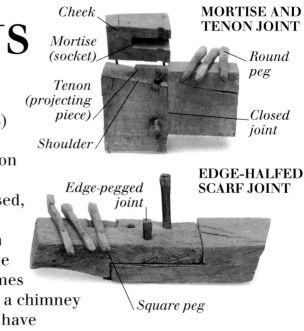

MORTISE AND TENON JOINT

Cheek · Mortise (socket) · Tenon (projecting piece) · Shoulder · Round peg · Closed joint

EDGE-HALFED SCARF JOINT

Edge-pegged joint · Square peg

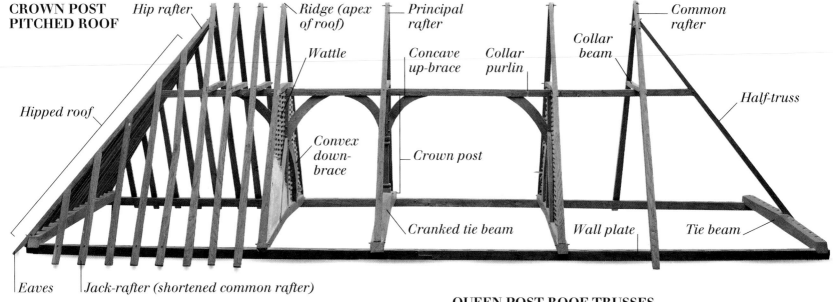

CROWN POST PITCHED ROOF

Hip rafter · Ridge (apex of roof) · Principal rafter · Common rafter · Collar beam · Wattle · Concave up-brace · Collar purlin · Half-truss · Hipped roof · Convex down-brace · Crown post · Cranked tie beam · Wall plate · Tie beam · Eaves · Jack-rafter (shortened common rafter)

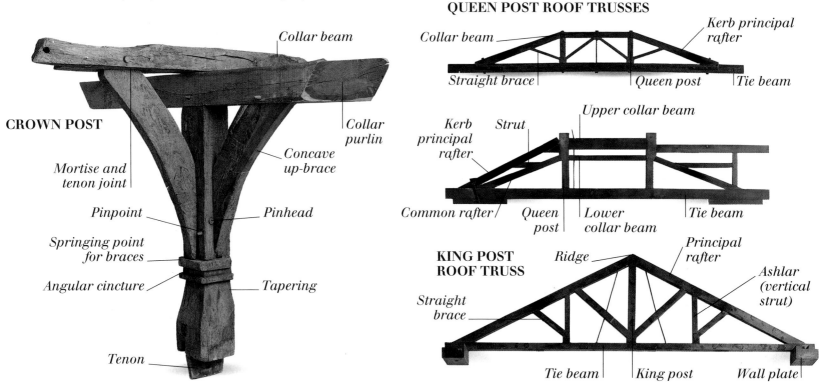

CROWN POST

Collar beam · Collar purlin · Concave up-brace · Mortise and tenon joint · Pinpoint · Pinhead · Springing point for braces · Angular cincture · Tapering · Tenon

QUEEN POST ROOF TRUSSES

Kerb principal rafter · Collar beam · Straight brace · Queen post · Tie beam

Upper collar beam · Kerb principal rafter · Strut · Common rafter · Queen post · Lower collar beam · Tie beam

KING POST ROOF TRUSS

Ridge · Principal rafter · Ashlar (vertical strut) · Straight brace · Tie beam · King post · Wall plate

TYPES OF ROOF

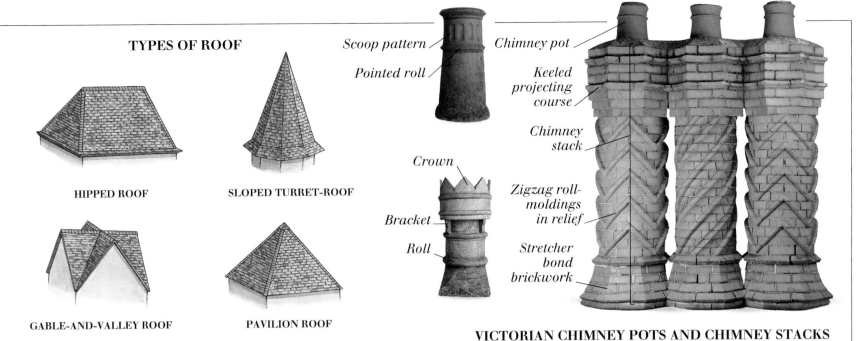

HIPPED ROOF

SLOPED TURRET-ROOF

GABLE-AND-VALLEY ROOF

PAVILION ROOF

Scoop pattern

Pointed roll

Chimney pot

Keeled projecting course

Chimney stack

Crown

Zigzag roll-moldings in relief

Bracket

Roll

Stretcher bond brickwork

VICTORIAN CHIMNEY POTS AND CHIMNEY STACKS

THATCHED ROOF

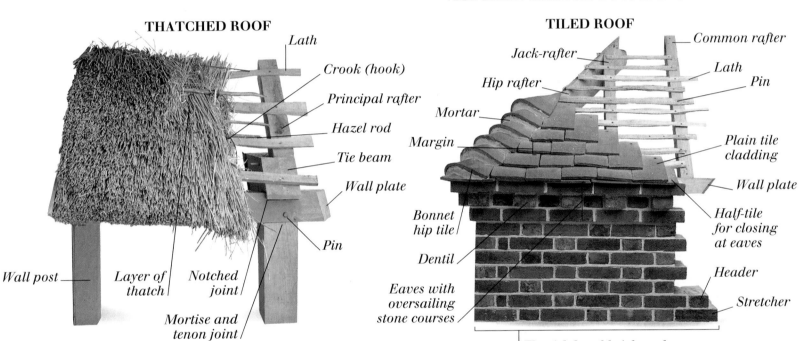

Lath

Crook (hook)

Principal rafter

Hazel rod

Tie beam

Wall plate

Pin

Wall post

Layer of thatch

Notched joint

Mortise and tenon joint

TILED ROOF

Jack-rafter

Hip rafter

Mortar

Margin

Bonnet hip tile

Dentil

Eaves with oversailing stone courses

Common rafter

Lath

Pin

Plain tile cladding

Wall plate

Half-tile for closing at eaves

Header

Stretcher

Flemish bond brickwork

TYPES OF ROOF TILE

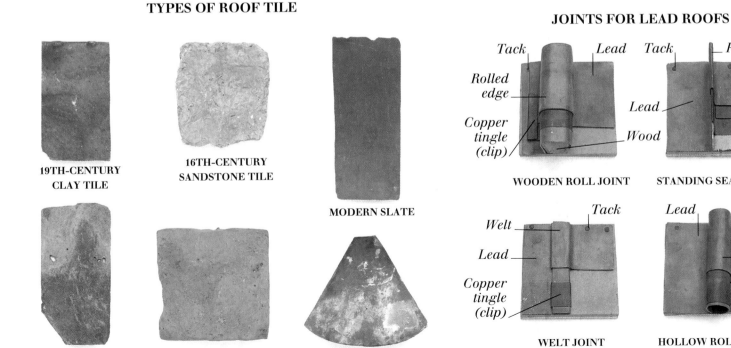

19TH-CENTURY CLAY TILE

16TH-CENTURY SANDSTONE TILE

MODERN SLATE

MODERN SLATE

ANCIENT ROMAN CLAY TILE

MODERN CLAY TILE

JOINTS FOR LEAD ROOFS

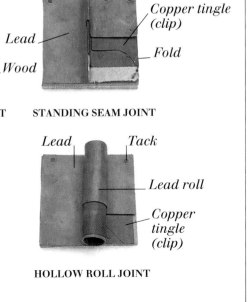

Tack

Lead

Rolled edge

Copper tingle (clip)

Wood

WOODEN ROLL JOINT

Tack

Folded edge

Copper tingle (clip)

Lead

Fold

STANDING SEAM JOINT

Welt

Lead

Copper tingle (clip)

Tack

WELT JOINT

Lead

Tack

Lead roll

Copper tingle (clip)

HOLLOW ROLL JOINT

Medieval castles and houses

WARFARE WAS COMMON IN EUROPE in the Middle Ages, and many monarchs and nobles built castles as a form of defense. Typical medieval castles have outer walls surrounding a moat. Inside the moat is a bailey (courtyard), protected by a chemise (jacket wall). The innermost and strongest part of a medieval castle is the keep. There are two main types of keep: towers called donjons, such as the Tour de César and Coucy-le-Château in France, and rectangular keeps ("hall-keeps"), such as the Tower of London. Castles were often guarded by salients (projecting fortifications), like those of the Bastille. Medieval houses typically had timber cruck (tent-like) frames, wattle-and-daub walls (see pp. 14-15), and pitched roofs, like those on medieval London Bridge (opposite).

DONJON, TOUR DE CESAR, PROVINS, FRANCE, 12TH CENTURY

Oculus
Battlements (crenellations)
Loophole
Conical spire
Hemispherical cupola
Gallery
Flying buttress
Squinch
Hexahedral hall
Vaulted room
Semicircular turret
Main entrance
Fireplace
Staircase to chemise (jacket wall)
Bailey
Embrasure
Chemise (jacket wall)
Plain impost
Depressed cupola
Vaulted staircase
Motte

Loophole

SALIENT, CAERNARVON CASTLE, BRITAIN, 1283-1325

Timber cruck frame

CRUCK-FRAMED HOUSE, BRITAIN, c.1200

Blind, rounded relieving arch
Merlon
Battlements (crenellations)
Tetrahedral spire
Crenel
Loophole
Rectangular turret
Wooden staircase leading to entrance above ground level
Quoin
Timber-framed house
Cornice
Buttress
Round-arched window with twin openings
Cruck frame
Paling

TOWER OF LONDON, BRITAIN, FROM 1070

Curtain wall
Pointed relieving arch
Semicircular relieving arch
Plain string course
Bracket decorated with scroll molding

Rectangular window
Sunken rectangular panel
Round-arched window
Semicircular salient
Loophole
Lateral circular salient

THE BASTILLE, PARIS, FRANCE, 14TH CENTURY

MEDIEVAL LONDON BRIDGE, BRITAIN, 1176 (WITH 14TH-CENTURY BATTLEMENTED BUILDING, NONESUCH HOUSE, AND TWO-TOWERED GATE)

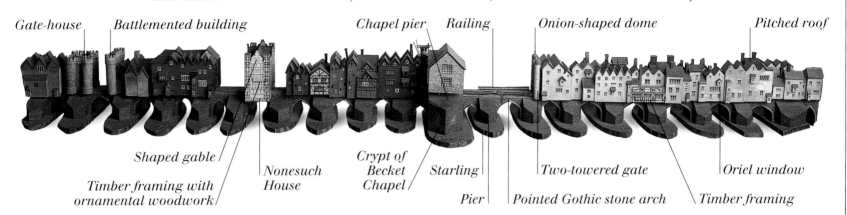

Gate-house   Battlemented building   Chapel pier   Railing   Onion-shaped dome   Pitched roof

Shaped gable   Nonesuch House   Crypt of Becket Chapel   Starling   Two-towered gate   Oriel window

Timber framing with ornamental woodwork   Pier   Pointed Gothic stone arch   Timber framing

DONJON, COUCY-LE-CHATEAU, AISNE, FRANCE, 1225-1245

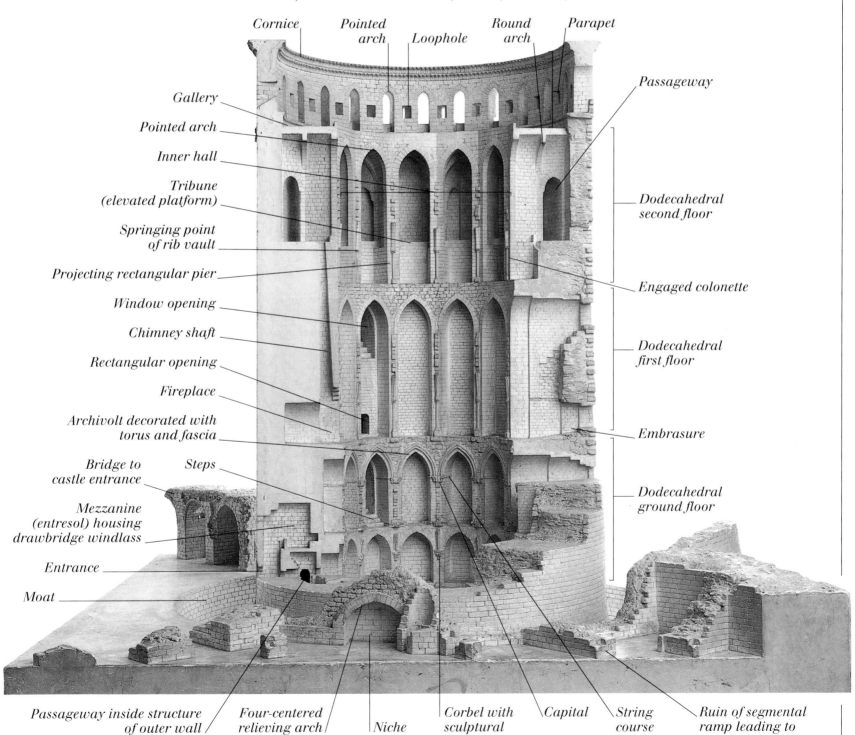

Cornice   Pointed arch   Loophole   Round arch   Parapet

Gallery   Passageway

Pointed arch

Inner hall

Tribune (elevated platform)   Dodecahedral second floor

Springing point of rib vault

Projecting rectangular pier   Engaged colonette

Window opening

Chimney shaft   Dodecahedral first floor

Rectangular opening

Fireplace

Archivolt decorated with torus and fascia   Embrasure

Bridge to castle entrance   Steps

Mezzanine (entresol) housing drawbridge windlass   Dodecahedral ground floor

Entrance

Moat

Passageway inside structure of outer wall   Four-centered relieving arch   Niche   Corbel with sculptural decoration   Capital   String course   Ruin of segmental ramp leading to chemise (jacket wall)

Medieval churches

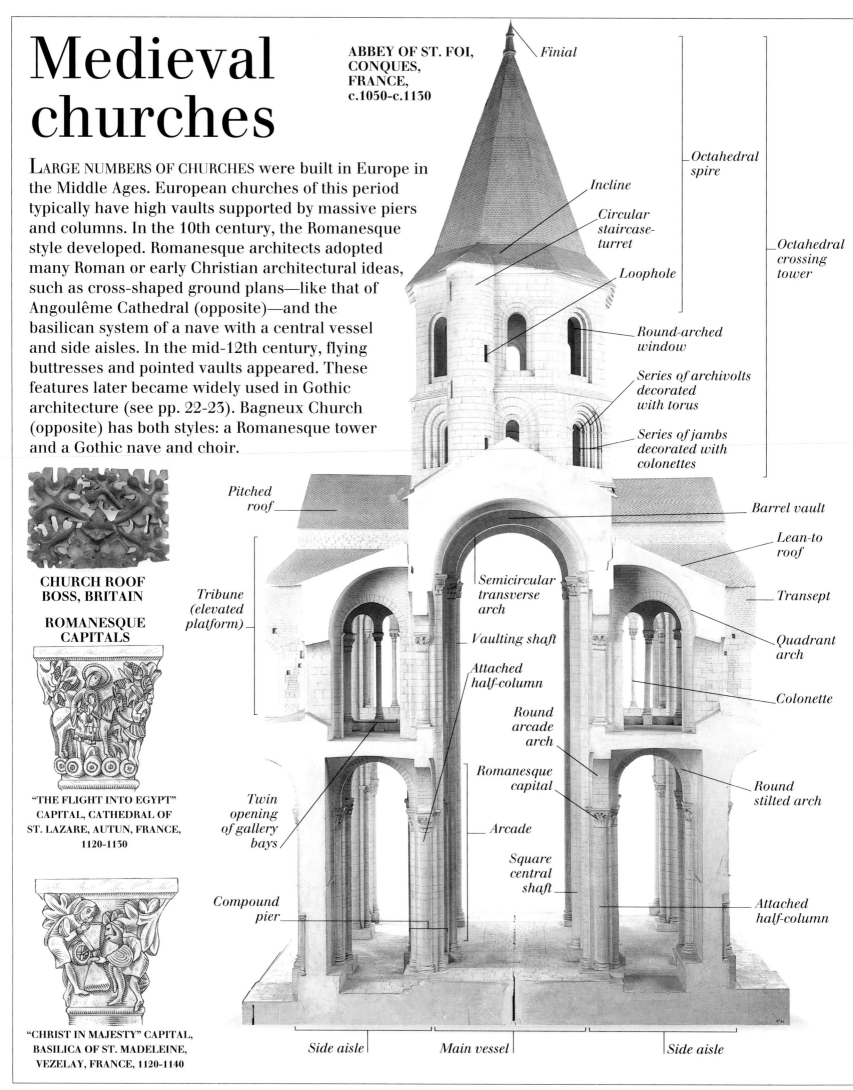

LARGE NUMBERS OF CHURCHES were built in Europe in the Middle Ages. European churches of this period typically have high vaults supported by massive piers and columns. In the 10th century, the Romanesque style developed. Romanesque architects adopted many Roman or early Christian architectural ideas, such as cross-shaped ground plans—like that of Angoulême Cathedral (opposite)—and the basilican system of a nave with a central vessel and side aisles. In the mid-12th century, flying buttresses and pointed vaults appeared. These features later became widely used in Gothic architecture (see pp. 22-23). Bagneux Church (opposite) has both styles: a Romanesque tower and a Gothic nave and choir.

ABBEY OF ST. FOI, CONQUES, FRANCE, c.1050-c.1130

Finial

Octahedral spire

Incline

Circular staircase-turret

Loophole

Round-arched window

Octahedral crossing tower

Series of archivolts decorated with torus

Series of jambs decorated with colonettes

CHURCH ROOF BOSS, BRITAIN

ROMANESQUE CAPITALS

"THE FLIGHT INTO EGYPT" CAPITAL, CATHEDRAL OF ST. LAZARE, AUTUN, FRANCE, 1120-1130

"CHRIST IN MAJESTY" CAPITAL, BASILICA OF ST. MADELEINE, VEZELAY, FRANCE, 1120-1140

Pitched roof

Tribune (elevated platform)

Twin opening of gallery bays

Compound pier

Semicircular transverse arch

Vaulting shaft

Attached half-column

Round arcade arch

Romanesque capital

Arcade

Square central shaft

Barrel vault

Lean-to roof

Transept

Quadrant arch

Colonette

Round stilted arch

Attached half-column

Side aisle | Main vessel | Side aisle

GROUND PLAN OF ANGOULEME CATHEDRAL, FRANCE, FROM c.1105

CHOIR, CHURCH OF ST. SERGE, ANGERS, FRANCE, c.1215-1220

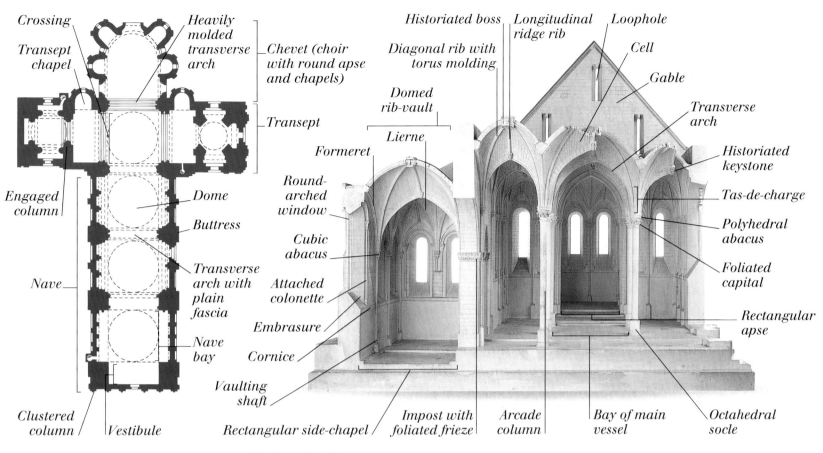

Crossing

Transept chapel

Heavily molded transverse arch

Chevet (choir with round apse and chapels)

Transept

Engaged column

Dome

Buttress

Nave

Transverse arch with plain fascia

Nave bay

Clustered column

Vestibule

Historiated boss

Diagonal rib with torus molding

Longitudinal ridge rib

Loophole

Cell

Gable

Transverse arch

Domed rib-vault

Lierne

Historiated keystone

Formeret

Tas-de-charge

Round-arched window

Polyhedral abacus

Cubic abacus

Foliated capital

Attached colonette

Rectangular apse

Embrasure

Cornice

Vaulting shaft

Rectangular side-chapel

Impost with foliated frieze

Arcade column

Bay of main vessel

Octahedral socle

BAGNEUX CHURCH, FRANCE, 1170-1190

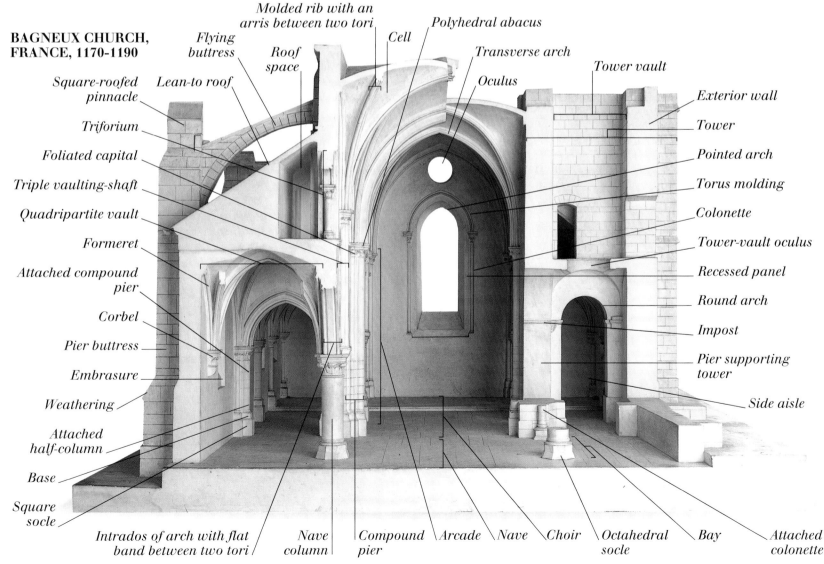

Molded rib with an arris between two tori

Flying buttress

Roof space

Cell

Polyhedral abacus

Transverse arch

Oculus

Tower vault

Square-roofed pinnacle

Lean-to roof

Exterior wall

Triforium

Tower

Foliated capital

Pointed arch

Triple vaulting-shaft

Torus molding

Quadripartite vault

Colonette

Formeret

Tower-vault oculus

Attached compound pier

Recessed panel

Corbel

Round arch

Pier buttress

Impost

Embrasure

Pier supporting tower

Weathering

Side aisle

Attached half-column

Base

Square socle

Intrados of arch with flat band between two tori

Nave column

Compound pier

Arcade

Nave

Choir

Octahedral socle

Bay

Attached colonette

Gothic 2

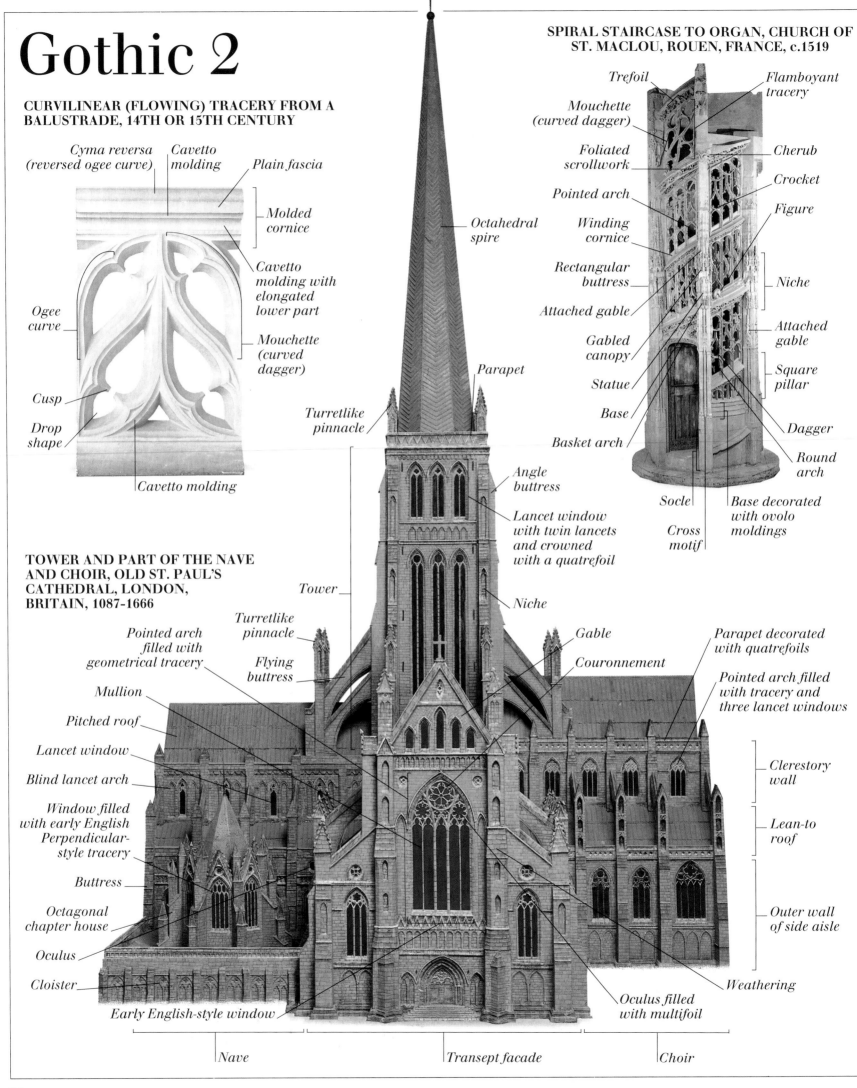

CURVILINEAR (FLOWING) TRACERY FROM A BALUSTRADE, 14TH OR 15TH CENTURY

Cyma reversa (reversed ogee curve)

Cavetto molding

Plain fascia

Molded cornice

Cavetto molding with elongated lower part

Ogee curve

Mouchette (curved dagger)

Cusp

Drop shape

Cavetto molding

SPIRAL STAIRCASE TO ORGAN, CHURCH OF ST. MACLOU, ROUEN, FRANCE, c.1519

Trefoil

Flamboyant tracery

Mouchette (curved dagger)

Cherub

Foliated scrollwork

Crocket

Pointed arch

Figure

Winding cornice

Rectangular buttress

Niche

Attached gable

Attached gable

Gabled canopy

Square pillar

Statue

Base

Dagger

Basket arch

Round arch

Socle

Base decorated with ovolo moldings

Cross motif

TOWER AND PART OF THE NAVE AND CHOIR, OLD ST. PAUL'S CATHEDRAL, LONDON, BRITAIN, 1087-1666

Octahedral spire

Parapet

Turretlike pinnacle

Angle buttress

Lancet window with twin lancets and crowned with a quatrefoil

Tower

Niche

Pointed arch filled with geometrical tracery

Turretlike pinnacle

Gable

Couronnement

Parapet decorated with quatrefoils

Flying buttress

Pointed arch filled with tracery and three lancet windows

Mullion

Pitched roof

Clerestory wall

Lancet window

Blind lancet arch

Lean-to roof

Window filled with early English Perpendicular-style tracery

Buttress

Outer wall of side aisle

Octagonal chapter house

Oculus

Cloister

Weathering

Early English-style window

Oculus filled with multifoil

Nave

Transept facade

Choir

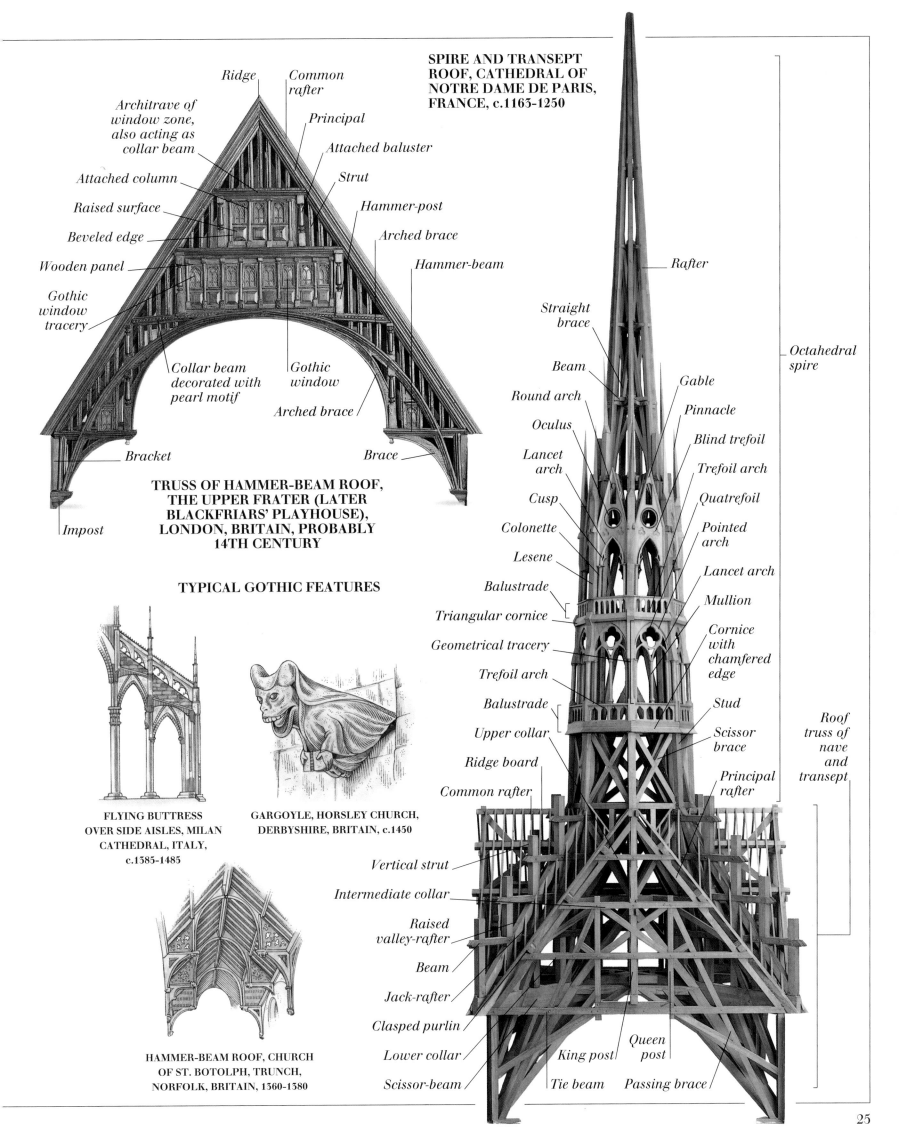

Ridge

Common rafter

Architrave of window zone, also acting as collar beam

Principal

Attached baluster

Attached column

Strut

Raised surface

Hammer-post

Beveled edge

Arched brace

Wooden panel

Hammer-beam

Gothic window tracery

Collar beam decorated with pearl motif

Gothic window

Arched brace

Bracket

Brace

Impost

TRUSS OF HAMMER-BEAM ROOF, THE UPPER FRATER (LATER BLACKFRIARS' PLAYHOUSE), LONDON, BRITAIN, PROBABLY 14TH CENTURY

TYPICAL GOTHIC FEATURES

FLYING BUTTRESS OVER SIDE AISLES, MILAN CATHEDRAL, ITALY, c.1385-1485

GARGOYLE, HORSLEY CHURCH, DERBYSHIRE, BRITAIN, c.1450

HAMMER-BEAM ROOF, CHURCH OF ST. BOTOLPH, TRUNCH, NORFOLK, BRITAIN, 1360-1380

SPIRE AND TRANSEPT ROOF, CATHEDRAL OF NOTRE DAME DE PARIS, FRANCE, c.1163-1250

Rafter

Straight brace

Beam

Gable

Round arch

Oculus

Pinnacle

Lancet arch

Blind trefoil

Cusp

Trefoil arch

Colonette

Quatrefoil

Lesene

Pointed arch

Balustrade

Lancet arch

Triangular cornice

Mullion

Geometrical tracery

Cornice with chamfered edge

Trefoil arch

Balustrade

Stud

Upper collar

Scissor brace

Ridge board

Principal rafter

Common rafter

Vertical strut

Intermediate collar

Raised valley-rafter

Beam

Jack-rafter

Clasped purlin

Queen post

Lower collar

King post

Scissor-beam

Tie beam

Passing brace

Octahedral spire

Roof truss of nave and transept

25

Renaissance 1

THE RENAISSANCE was a period in European history—lasting roughly from the 14th century to the mid-17th century—during which the arts and sciences underwent great changes. In architecture, these changes were marked by a return to the classical forms and proportions of ancient Roman buildings. The Renaissance originated in Italy, and the buildings most characteristic of its style can be found there, such as the Palazzo Strozzi shown here. Mannerism is a branch of the Renaissance style that distorts the classical forms; an example is the Laurentian Library staircase. As the Renaissance style spread to other European countries, many of its features were incorporated into the local architecture. For example, the Château de Montal in France (see pp. 28-29) incorporates aedicules (tabernacles).

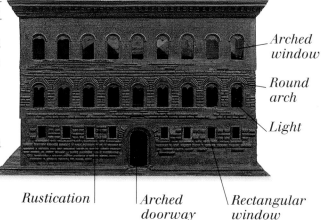

Crowning cornice

Arched window

Round arch

Light

Rustication

Arched doorway

Rectangular window

SIDE VIEW OF PALAZZO STROZZI, FLORENCE, ITALY, 1489 (BY G. DA SANGALLO, B. DA MAIANO, AND CRONACA)

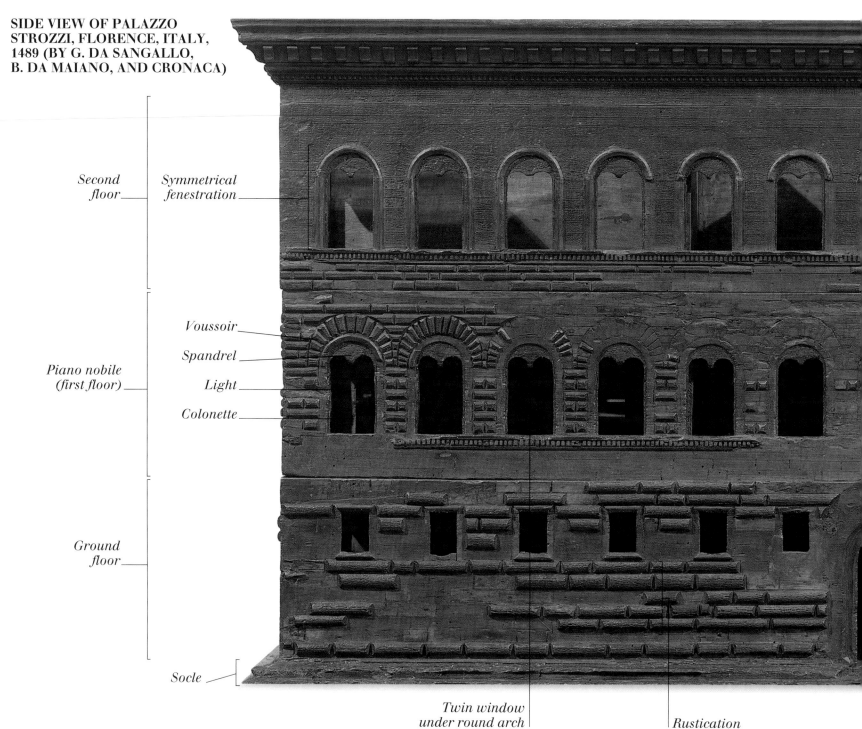

Second floor

Symmetrical fenestration

Voussoir

Spandrel

Light

Colonette

Piano nobile (first floor)

Ground floor

Socle

Twin window under round arch

Rustication

DETAILS FROM ITALIAN RENAISSANCE BUILDINGS

**PANEL FROM DRUM OF DOME,
FLORENCE CATHEDRAL, 1420-1436**

**COFFERING IN DOME,
PAZZI CHAPEL,
FLORENCE, 1429-1461**

**STAIRCASE,
LAURENTIAN LIBRARY,
FLORENCE, 1559**

**PORTICO, VILLA ROTUNDA,
VICENZA, 1567-1569**

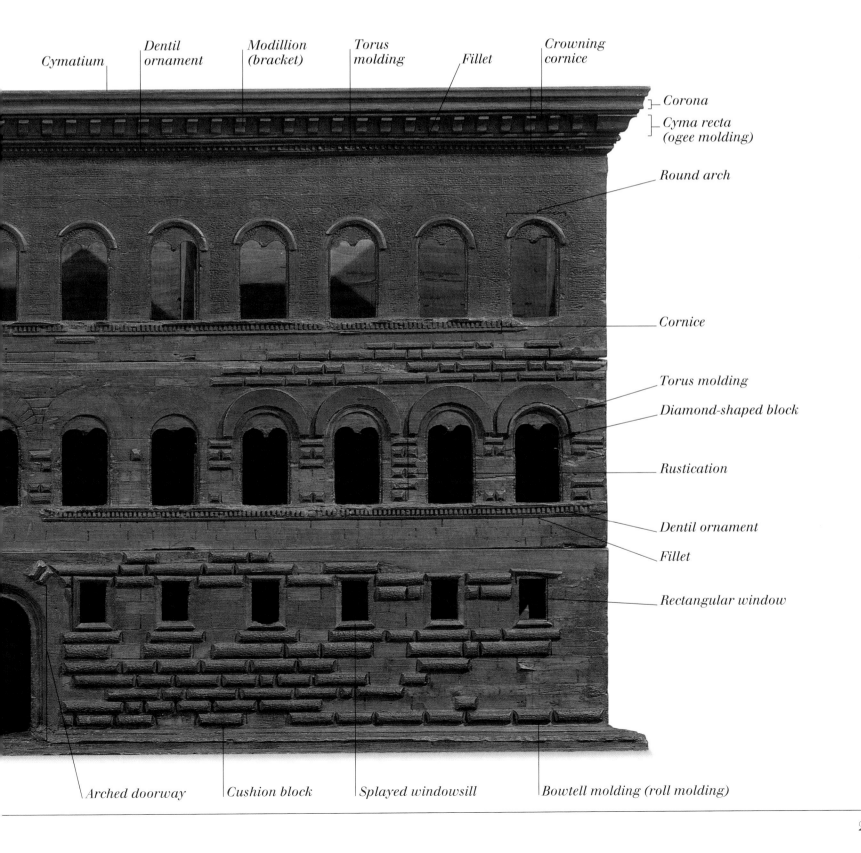

Cymatium

Dentil ornament

Modillion (bracket)

Torus molding

Fillet

Crowning cornice

Corona

Cyma recta (ogee molding)

Round arch

Cornice

Torus molding

Diamond-shaped block

Rustication

Dentil ornament

Fillet

Rectangular window

Arched doorway

Cushion block

Splayed windowsill

Bowtell molding (roll molding)

Renaissance 2

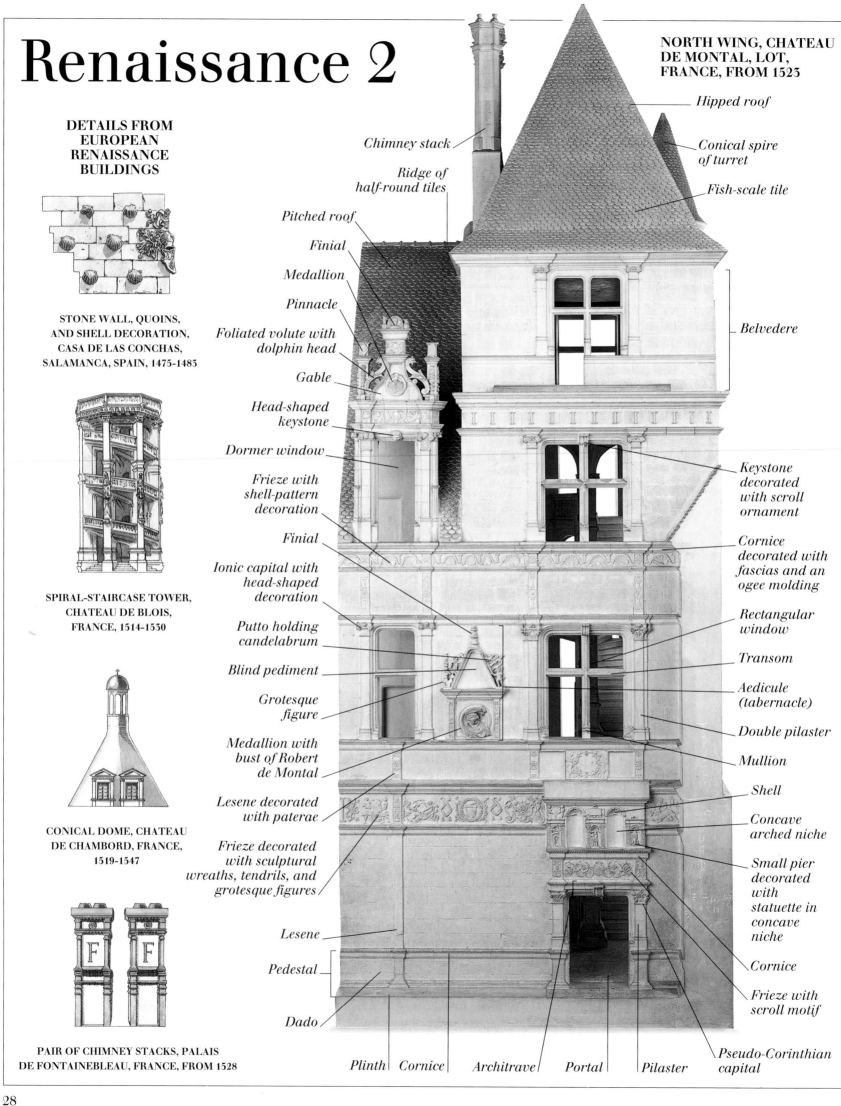

DETAILS FROM EUROPEAN RENAISSANCE BUILDINGS

STONE WALL, QUOINS, AND SHELL DECORATION, CASA DE LAS CONCHAS, SALAMANCA, SPAIN, 1475-1483

SPIRAL-STAIRCASE TOWER, CHATEAU DE BLOIS, FRANCE, 1514-1550

CONICAL DOME, CHATEAU DE CHAMBORD, FRANCE, 1519-1547

PAIR OF CHIMNEY STACKS, PALAIS DE FONTAINEBLEAU, FRANCE, FROM 1528

Hipped roof

Conical spire of turret

Fish-scale tile

Chimney stack

Ridge of half-round tiles

Pitched roof

Finial

Medallion

Pinnacle

Foliated volute with dolphin head

Gable

Head-shaped keystone

Dormer window

Frieze with shell-pattern decoration

Finial

Ionic capital with head-shaped decoration

Putto holding candelabrum

Blind pediment

Grotesque figure

Medallion with bust of Robert de Montal

Lesene decorated with paterae

Frieze decorated with sculptural wreaths, tendrils, and grotesque figures

Lesene

Pedestal

Dado

Belvedere

Keystone decorated with scroll ornament

Cornice decorated with fascias and an ogee molding

Rectangular window

Transom

Aedicule (tabernacle)

Double pilaster

Mullion

Shell

Concave arched niche

Small pier decorated with statuette in concave niche

Cornice

Frieze with scroll motif

Pseudo-Corinthian capital

Plinth   Cornice   Architrave   Portal   Pilaster

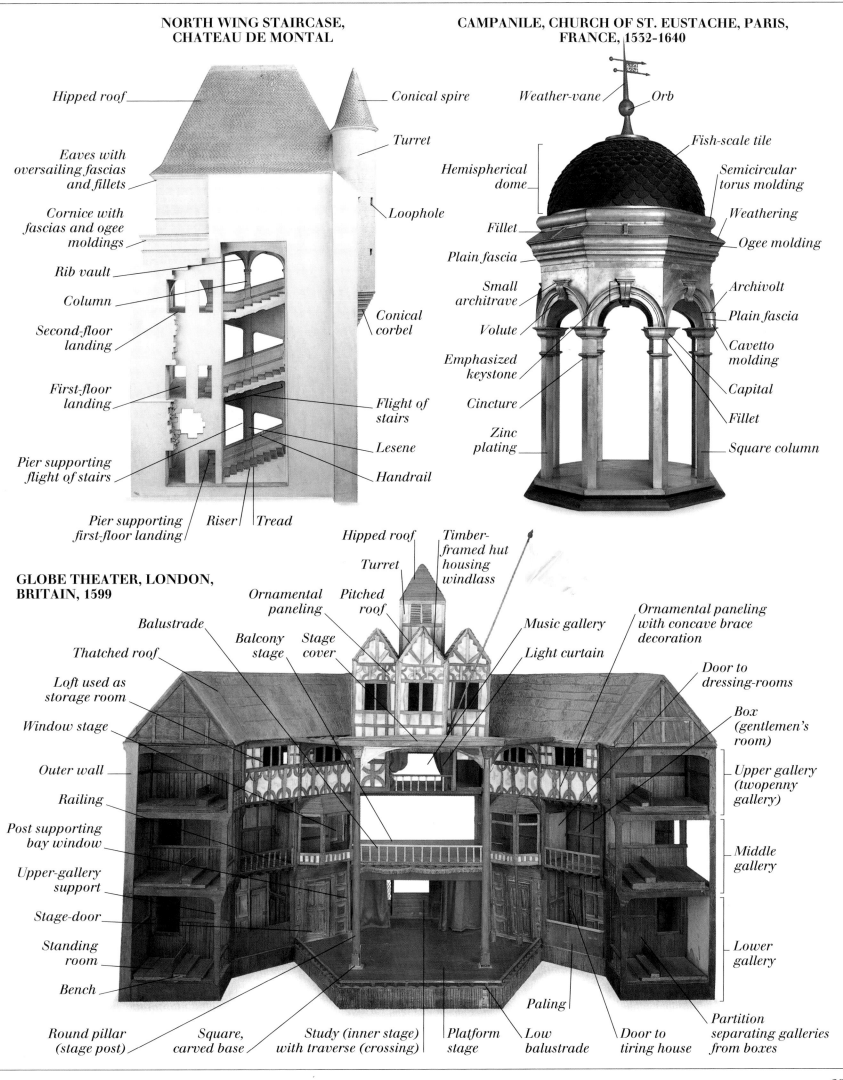

NORTH WING STAIRCASE, CHATEAU DE MONTAL

Hipped roof

Eaves with oversailing fascias and fillets

Cornice with fascias and ogee moldings

Rib vault

Column

Second-floor landing

First-floor landing

Pier supporting flight of stairs

Pier supporting first-floor landing

Riser

Tread

Conical spire

Turret

Loophole

Conical corbel

Flight of stairs

Lesene

Handrail

CAMPANILE, CHURCH OF ST. EUSTACHE, PARIS, FRANCE, 1532-1640

Weather-vane

Orb

Fish-scale tile

Hemispherical dome

Semicircular torus molding

Weathering

Ogee molding

Fillet

Plain fascia

Small architrave

Archivolt

Plain fascia

Volute

Cavetto molding

Emphasized keystone

Capital

Cincture

Fillet

Zinc plating

Square column

GLOBE THEATER, LONDON, BRITAIN, 1599

Balustrade

Thatched roof

Loft used as storage room

Window stage

Outer wall

Railing

Post supporting bay window

Upper-gallery support

Stage-door

Standing room

Bench

Round pillar (stage post)

Square, carved base

Hipped roof

Turret

Ornamental paneling

Balcony stage

Pitched roof

Stage cover

Timber-framed hut housing windlass

Music gallery

Light curtain

Ornamental paneling with concave brace decoration

Door to dressing-rooms

Box (gentlemen's room)

Upper gallery (twopenny gallery)

Middle gallery

Lower gallery

Study (inner stage) with traverse (crossing)

Platform stage

Paling

Low balustrade

Door to tiring house

Partition separating galleries from boxes

29

Baroque and neoclassical 1

THE BAROQUE STYLE EVOLVED IN THE EARLY 17TH CENTURY in Rome. It is characterized by curved outlines and ostentatious decoration, as can be seen in the Italian church details (right). The baroque style was particularly widely favored in Italy, Spain, and Germany. It was also adopted in Britain and France, but with adaptations. The British architects Christopher Wren and Nicholas Hawksmoor, for example, used baroque features—such as the concave walls of St. Paul's Cathedral and the curved buttresses of the Church of St. George in the East (see pp. 32-33)—but they did so with restraint. Similarly, the curved buttresses and volutes of the Parisian Church of St. Paul-St. Louis are relatively plain. In the second half of the 17th century, a distinct classical style (known as neoclassicism) developed in northern Europe as a reaction to the excesses of baroque. Typical of this new style were churches such as the Madeleine (a proposed facade is shown below), as well as secular buildings such as the Cirque Napoleon (opposite) and the buildings of the British architect Sir John Soane (see pp. 34-35). In early 18th century France, an extremely lavish form of baroque developed, known as rococo. The balcony from Nantes (see pp. 34-35) with its twisted ironwork and head-shaped corbels is typical of this style.

SCROLLED BUTTRESS, CHURCH OF ST. MARIA DELLA SALUTE, VENICE, 1631-1682

STATUE OF THE ECSTASY OF ST. THERESA, CHURCH OF ST. MARIA DELLA VITTORIA, ROME, 1645-1652

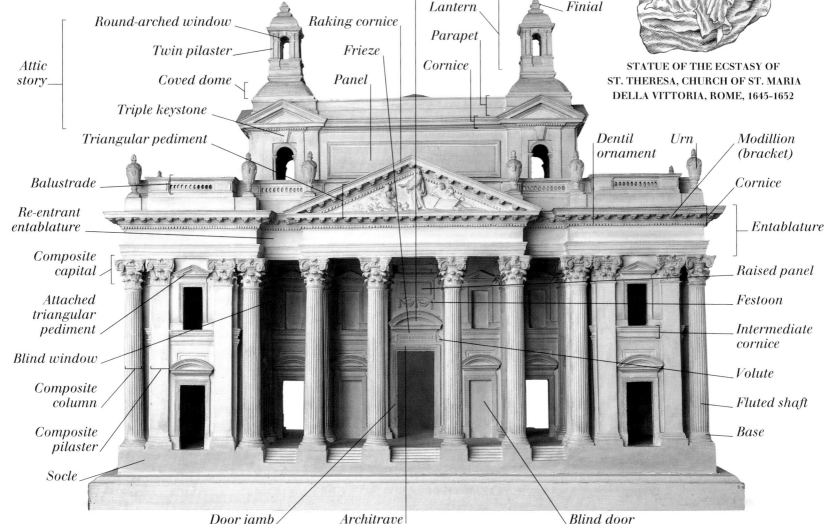

PROPOSED FACADE, THE MADELEINE (NEOCLASSICAL), PARIS, FRANCE, 1764 (BY P. CONTANT D'IVRY)

CIRQUE NAPOLEON (NEOCLASSICAL), PARIS, FRANCE, 1852 (BY J.I. HITTORFF)

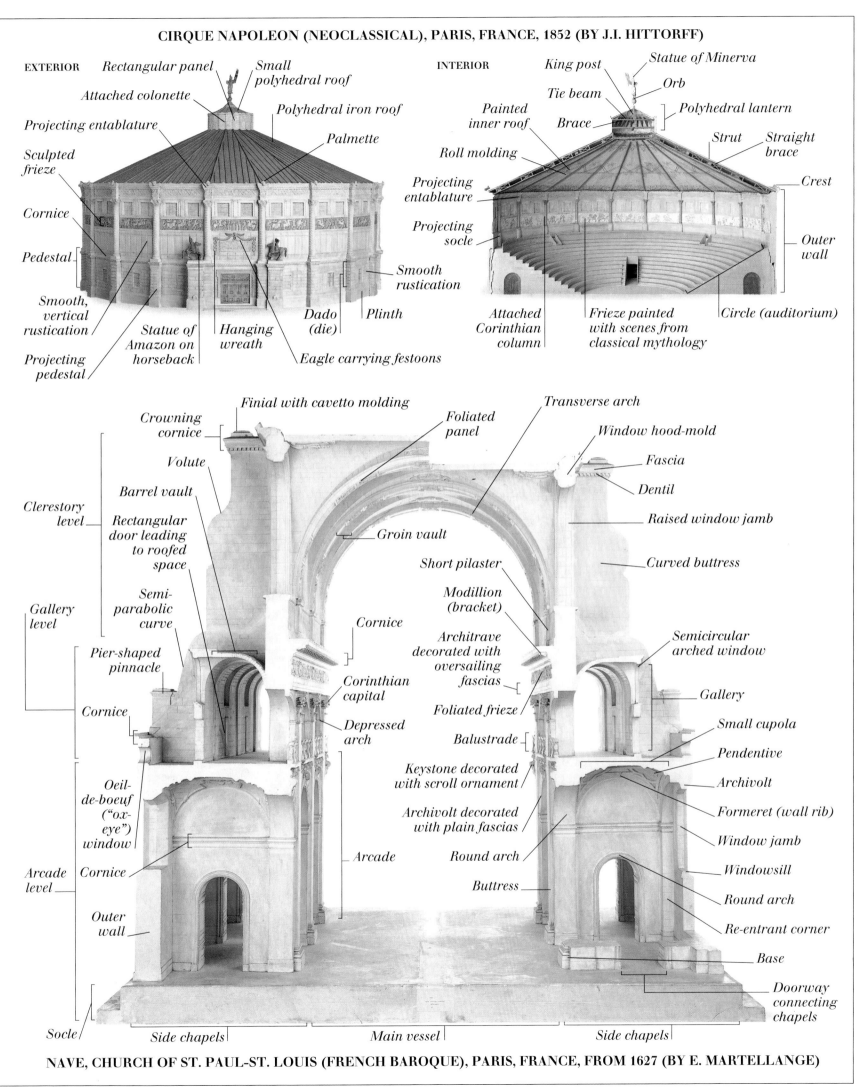

EXTERIOR

Rectangular panel
Small polyhedral roof
Attached colonette
Polyhedral iron roof
Projecting entablature
Palmette
Sculpted frieze
Cornice
Pedestal
Smooth, vertical rustication
Smooth rustication
Statue of Amazon on horseback
Hanging wreath
Dado (die)
Plinth
Projecting pedestal
Eagle carrying festoons

INTERIOR

King post
Statue of Minerva
Tie beam
Orb
Painted inner roof
Brace
Polyhedral lantern
Roll molding
Strut
Straight brace
Projecting entablature
Crest
Projecting socle
Outer wall
Attached Corinthian column
Frieze painted with scenes from classical mythology
Circle (auditorium)

Finial with cavetto molding
Transverse arch
Crowning cornice
Foliated panel
Window hood-mold
Volute
Fascia
Clerestory level
Dentil
Rectangular door leading to roofed space
Barrel vault
Raised window jamb
Groin vault
Curved buttress
Gallery level
Short pilaster
Semi-parabolic curve
Cornice
Modillion (bracket)
Semicircular arched window
Pier-shaped pinnacle
Architrave decorated with oversailing fascias
Corinthian capital
Gallery
Cornice
Foliated frieze
Depressed arch
Small cupola
Oeil-de-boeuf ("ox-eye") window
Balustrade
Pendentive
Keystone decorated with scroll ornament
Archivolt
Arcade level
Cornice
Formeret (wall rib)
Archivolt decorated with plain fascias
Window jamb
Outer wall
Arcade
Round arch
Windowsill
Buttress
Round arch
Re-entrant corner
Base
Doorway connecting chapels
Socle
Side chapels
Main vessel
Side chapels

NAVE, CHURCH OF ST. PAUL-ST. LOUIS (FRENCH BAROQUE), PARIS, FRANCE, FROM 1627 (BY E. MARTELLANGE)

Baroque and neoclassical 2

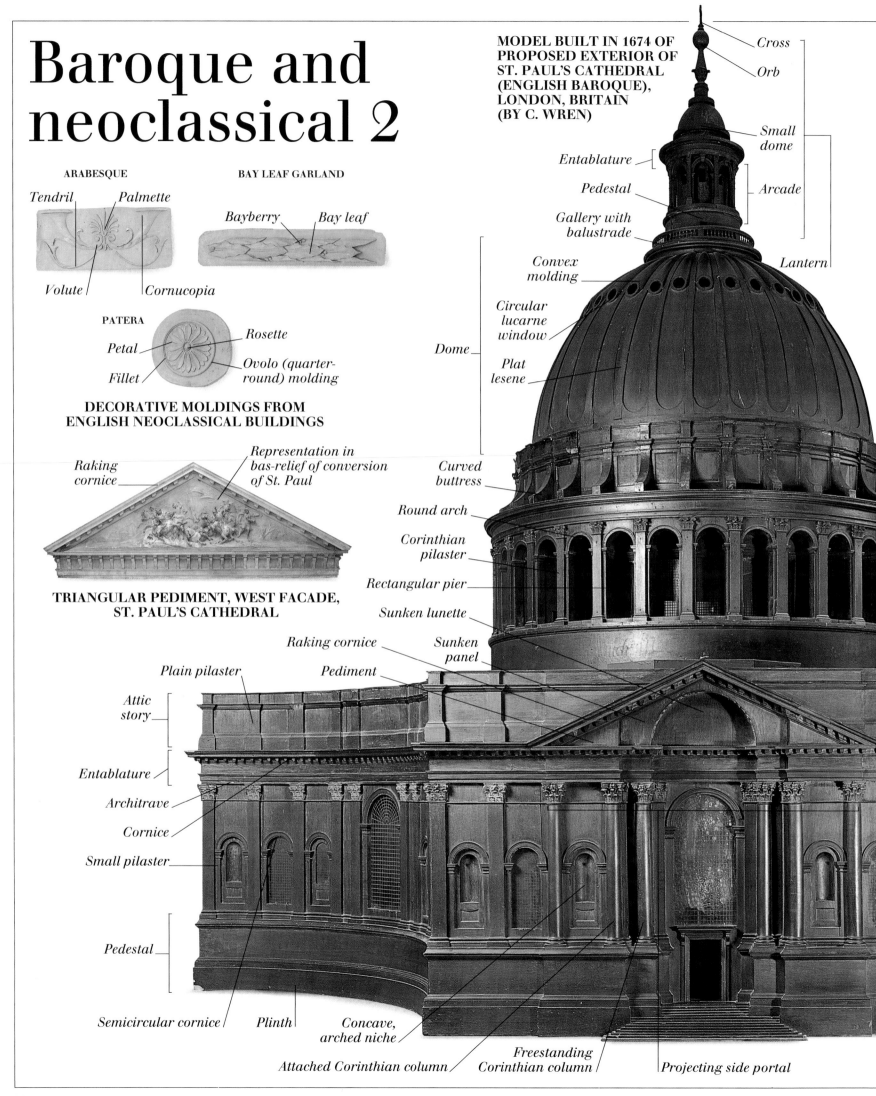

ARABESQUE

Tendril
Palmette
Volute
Cornucopia

BAY LEAF GARLAND

Bayberry
Bay leaf

PATERA

Petal
Fillet
Rosette
Ovolo (quarter-round) molding

DECORATIVE MOLDINGS FROM ENGLISH NEOCLASSICAL BUILDINGS

Raking cornice
Representation in bas-relief of conversion of St. Paul

TRIANGULAR PEDIMENT, WEST FACADE, ST. PAUL'S CATHEDRAL

Plain pilaster
Attic story
Entablature
Architrave
Cornice
Small pilaster
Pedestal
Semicircular cornice
Plinth
Concave, arched niche
Attached Corinthian column
Freestanding Corinthian column
Projecting side portal

Raking cornice
Pediment

MODEL BUILT IN 1674 OF PROPOSED EXTERIOR OF ST. PAUL'S CATHEDRAL (ENGLISH BAROQUE), LONDON, BRITAIN (BY C. WREN)

Cross
Orb
Small dome
Entablature
Pedestal
Arcade
Gallery with balustrade
Convex molding
Lantern
Circular lucarne window
Dome
Plat lesene
Curved buttress
Round arch
Corinthian pilaster
Rectangular pier
Sunken lunette
Sunken panel

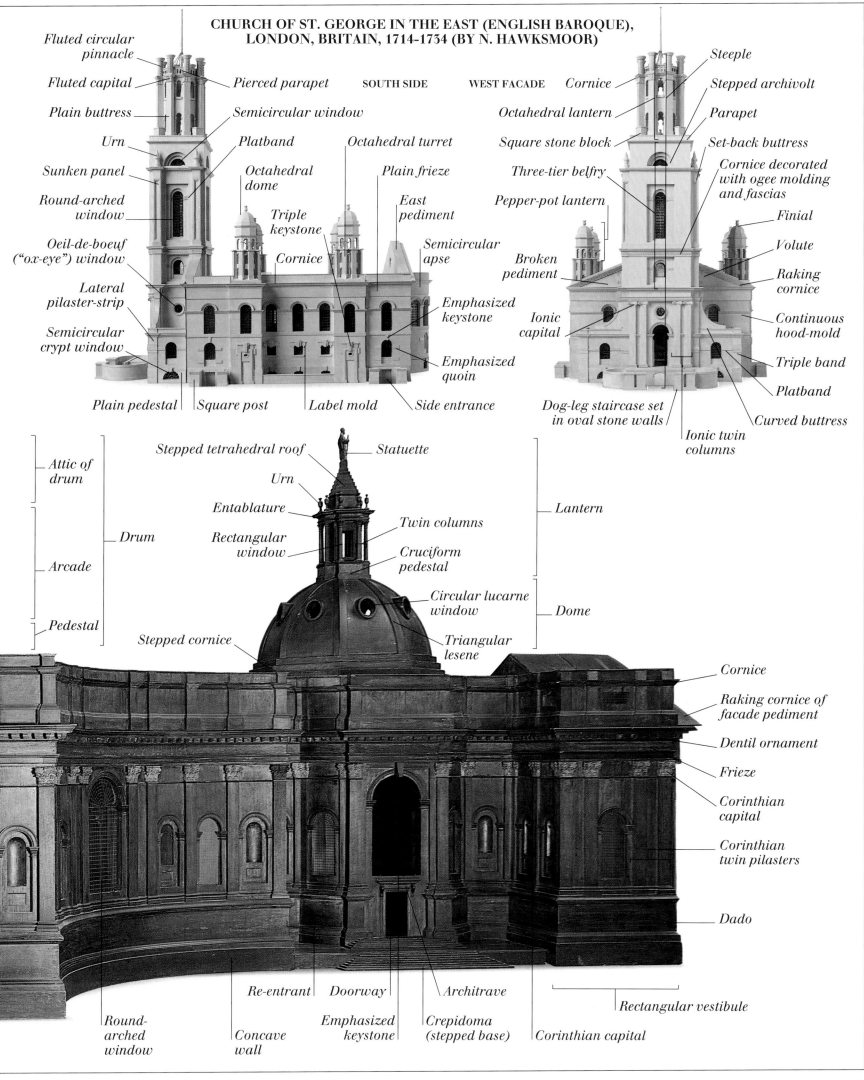

CHURCH OF ST. GEORGE IN THE EAST (ENGLISH BAROQUE), LONDON, BRITAIN, 1714-1734 (BY N. HAWKSMOOR)

SOUTH SIDE WEST FACADE

Fluted circular pinnacle

Fluted capital

Plain buttress

Urn

Sunken panel

Round-arched window

Oeil-de-boeuf ("ox-eye") window

Lateral pilaster-strip

Semicircular crypt window

Pierced parapet

Semicircular window

Platband

Octahedral dome

Triple keystone

Cornice

Octahedral turret

Plain frieze

East pediment

Semicircular apse

Emphasized keystone

Emphasized quoin

Plain pedestal

Square post

Label mold

Side entrance

Steeple

Cornice

Octahedral lantern

Square stone block

Three-tier belfry

Pepper-pot lantern

Broken pediment

Ionic capital

Dog-leg staircase set in oval stone walls

Ionic twin columns

Stepped archivolt

Parapet

Set-back buttress

Cornice decorated with ogee molding and fascias

Finial

Volute

Raking cornice

Continuous hood-mold

Triple band

Platband

Curved buttress

Attic of drum

Drum

Arcade

Pedestal

Stepped tetrahedral roof

Urn

Entablature

Rectangular window

Stepped cornice

Statuette

Twin columns

Cruciform pedestal

Circular lucarne window

Triangular lesene

Lantern

Dome

Cornice

Raking cornice of facade pediment

Dentil ornament

Frieze

Corinthian capital

Corinthian twin pilasters

Dado

Round-arched window

Concave wall

Re-entrant

Emphasized keystone

Doorway

Crepidoma (stepped base)

Architrave

Corinthian capital

Rectangular vestibule

Baroque and neoclassical 3

DETAILS FROM BAROQUE, NEOCLASSICAL, AND ROCOCO BUILDINGS

PORTICO, THE VYNE, HAMPSHIRE, BRITAIN, 1654 (NEOCLASSICAL)

GILT IRONWORK FROM SCREEN, PALACE OF VERSAILLES, FRANCE, 1669-1674 (FRENCH BAROQUE)

WINDOW, PALAZZO STANGA, CREMONA, ITALY, EARLY 18TH CENTURY (ROCOCO)

ATLAS (MALE CARYATID), UPPER BELVEDERE, VIENNA, AUSTRIA, 1721 (GERMAN-STYLE BAROQUE)

BALCONY, NANTES, FRANCE, 1730-1740 (ROCOCO)

MASONRY OF A NICHE IN THE ROTUNDA (NEOCLASSICAL), BANK OF ENGLAND, LONDON, BRITAIN, 1794 (BY J. SOANE)

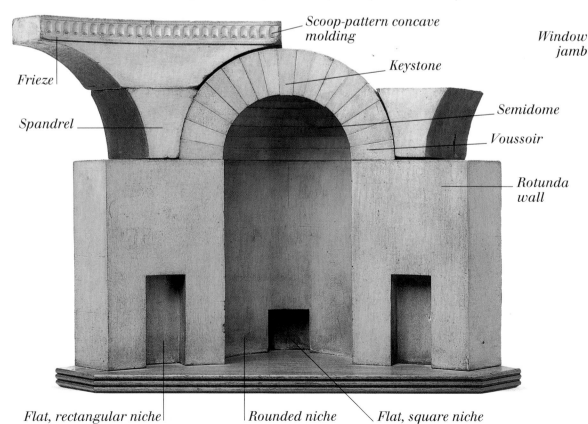

Scoop-pattern concave molding

Keystone

Frieze

Spandrel

Semidome

Voussoir

Rotunda wall

Flat, rectangular niche

Rounded niche

Flat, square niche

CORNER OF THE NEW STATE PAPER OFFICE (NEOCLASSICAL), LONDON, BRITAIN, 1830-1831 (BY J. SOANE)

Classical-style entablature

Pantile (S-shaped roofing tile)

Fascia

Curved corbel

Smooth rustication

Cornice

Window jamb

Cornice

Frieze

Architrave

Eaves

Scroll-shaped corbel

Second-floor window

Drip-cap

Cornice

Frieze

Window architrave

First-floor window

Windowsill in the form of a frieze

Ground-floor window

Splayed windowsill

Vermiculated rustication

TYRINGHAM HOUSE (NEOCLASSICAL), BUCKINGHAMSHIRE, BRITAIN, 1793-1797 (BY J. SOANE)

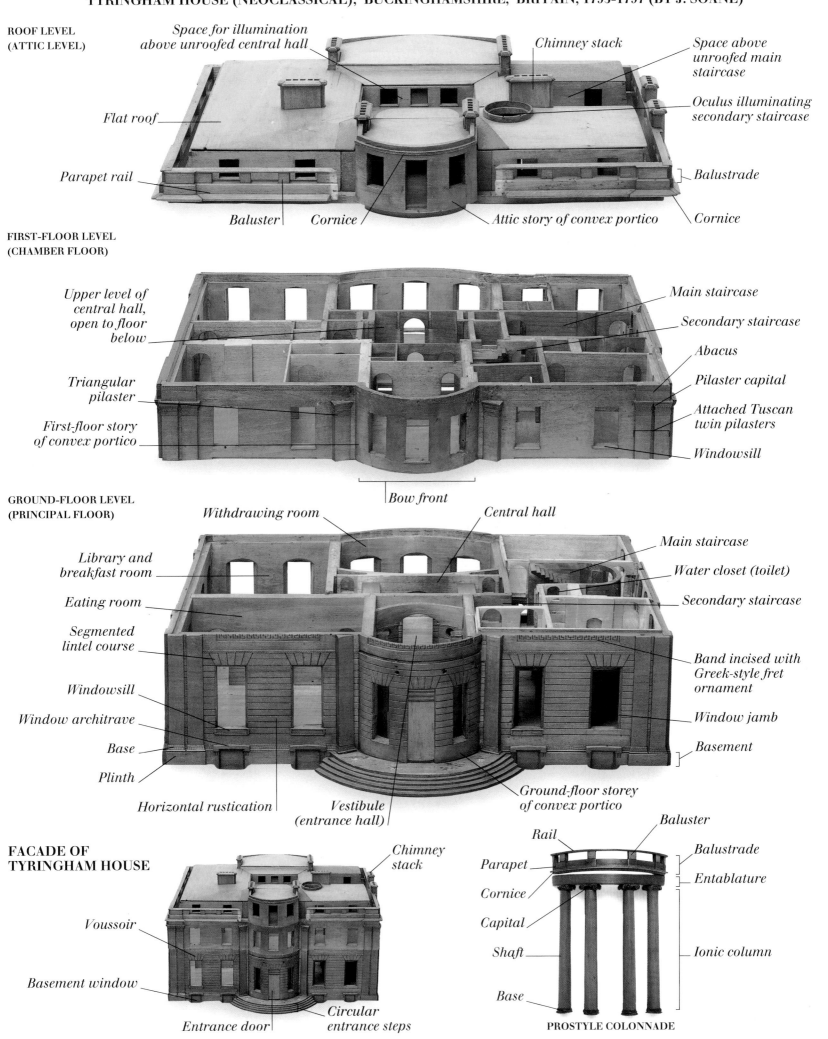

ROOF LEVEL (ATTIC LEVEL)

Space for illumination above unroofed central hall

Chimney stack

Space above unroofed main staircase

Oculus illuminating secondary staircase

Flat roof

Parapet rail

Balustrade

Cornice

Baluster

Cornice

Attic story of convex portico

FIRST-FLOOR LEVEL (CHAMBER FLOOR)

Upper level of central hall, open to floor below

Main staircase

Secondary staircase

Abacus

Pilaster capital

Triangular pilaster

Attached Tuscan twin pilasters

First-floor story of convex portico

Windowsill

Bow front

GROUND-FLOOR LEVEL (PRINCIPAL FLOOR)

Withdrawing room

Central hall

Main staircase

Library and breakfast room

Water closet (toilet)

Eating room

Secondary staircase

Segmented lintel course

Band incised with Greek-style fret ornament

Windowsill

Window architrave

Window jamb

Base

Basement

Plinth

Horizontal rustication

Vestibule (entrance hall)

Ground-floor storey of convex portico

FACADE OF TYRINGHAM HOUSE

Chimney stack

Voussoir

Basement window

Entrance door

Circular entrance steps

Rail

Baluster

Parapet

Balustrade

Cornice

Entablature

Capital

Shaft

Ionic column

Base

PROSTYLE COLONNADE

Ceilings

EARLY CEILINGS WERE SIMPLY the underside of the floor above with the timbers exposed. By the 16th century, the timbers were covered with boards and stucco (plaster). Molded stucco ceilings became popular during the 17th century. Some were elaborately ornamented, such as the one shown here. Even today, board-and-plaster ceilings are commonly used in new buildings.

Scrolled petal — *Stylized stamen*

PATERA (ROSETTE)

MIDDLE PANELS: TRIUMPHAL PROCESSION OF CHERUBS (TOP AND BOTTOM); GLORIFICATION OF JAMES I (CENTER)

MOLDED STUCCO CEILING, THE BANQUETING HOUSE, WHITEHALL PALACE, LONDON, BRITAIN, 1666-1693 (DESIGNED BY I. JONES, PAINTED BY P.P. RUBENS)

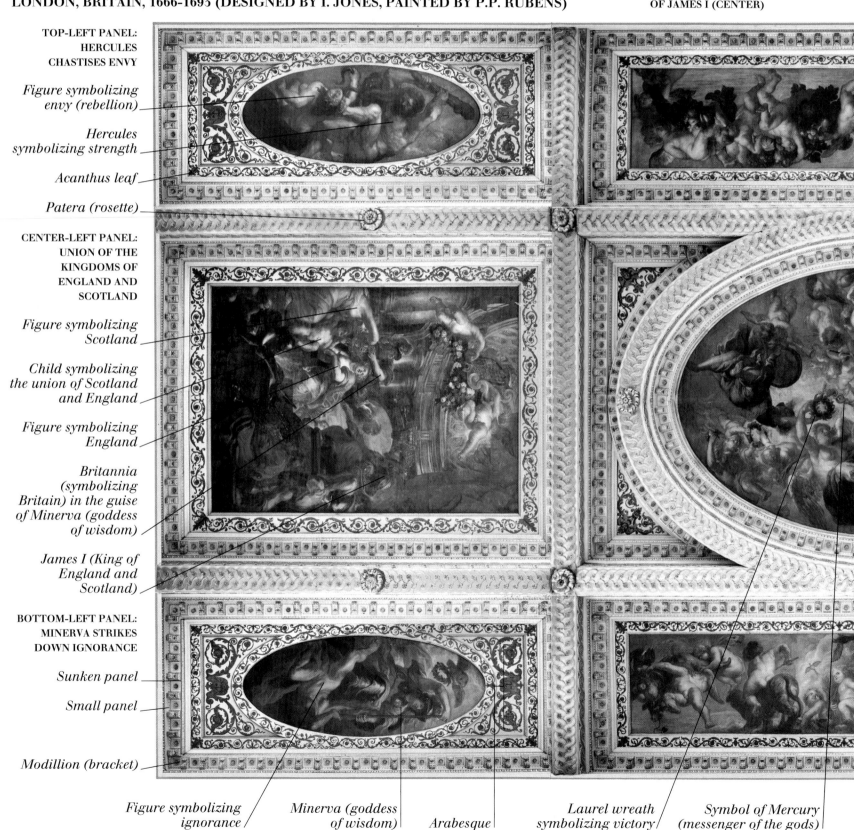

TOP-LEFT PANEL: HERCULES CHASTISES ENVY

Figure symbolizing envy (rebellion)

Hercules symbolizing strength

Acanthus leaf

Patera (rosette)

CENTER-LEFT PANEL: UNION OF THE KINGDOMS OF ENGLAND AND SCOTLAND

Figure symbolizing Scotland

Child symbolizing the union of Scotland and England

Figure symbolizing England

Britannia (symbolizing Britain) in the guise of Minerva (goddess of wisdom)

James I (King of England and Scotland)

BOTTOM-LEFT PANEL: MINERVA STRIKES DOWN IGNORANCE

Sunken panel

Small panel

Modillion (bracket)

Figure symbolizing ignorance

Minerva (goddess of wisdom)

Arabesque

Laurel wreath symbolizing victory

Symbol of Mercury (messenger of the gods)

DETAILS OF MOLDED STUCCO FROM THE BANQUETING HOUSE CEILING

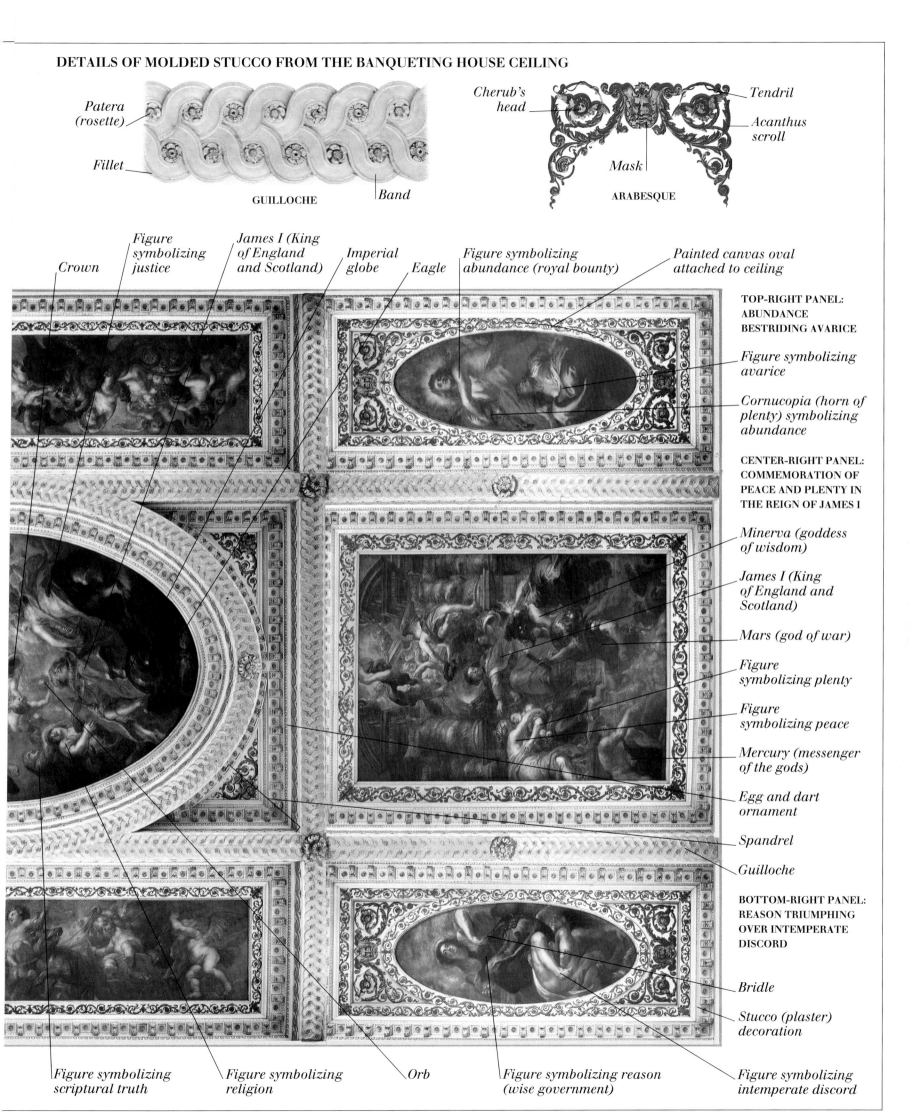

Patera (rosette)

Fillet

Band

GUILLOCHE

Cherub's head

Tendril

Acanthus scroll

Mask

ARABESQUE

Crown

Figure symbolizing justice

James I (King of England and Scotland)

Imperial globe

Eagle

Figure symbolizing abundance (royal bounty)

Painted canvas oval attached to ceiling

TOP-RIGHT PANEL: ABUNDANCE BESTRIDING AVARICE

Figure symbolizing avarice

Cornucopia (horn of plenty) symbolizing abundance

CENTER-RIGHT PANEL: COMMEMORATION OF PEACE AND PLENTY IN THE REIGN OF JAMES I

Minerva (goddess of wisdom)

James I (King of England and Scotland)

Mars (god of war)

Figure symbolizing plenty

Figure symbolizing peace

Mercury (messenger of the gods)

Egg and dart ornament

Spandrel

Guilloche

BOTTOM-RIGHT PANEL: REASON TRIUMPHING OVER INTEMPERATE DISCORD

Bridle

Stucco (plaster) decoration

Figure symbolizing scriptural truth

Figure symbolizing religion

Orb

Figure symbolizing reason (wise government)

Figure symbolizing intemperate discord

37

Domes

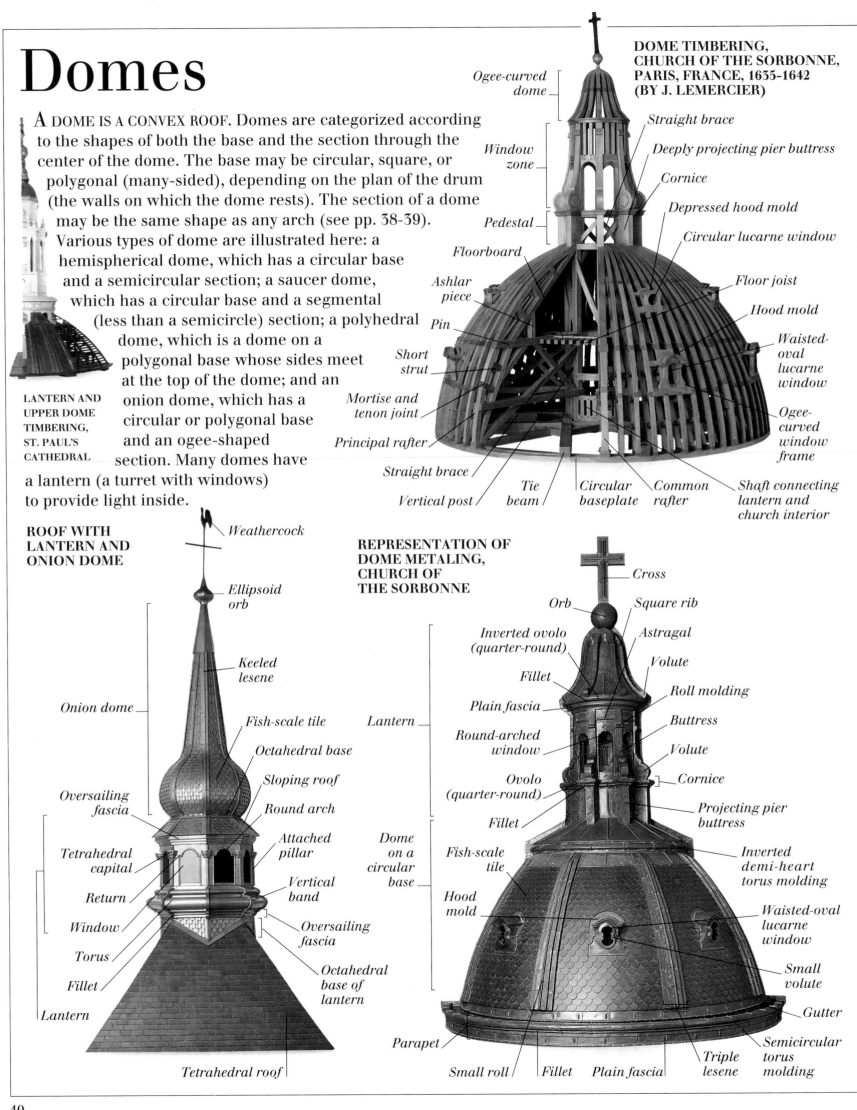

A DOME IS A CONVEX ROOF. Domes are categorized according to the shapes of both the base and the section through the center of the dome. The base may be circular, square, or polygonal (many-sided), depending on the plan of the drum (the walls on which the dome rests). The section of a dome may be the same shape as any arch (see pp. 38-39). Various types of dome are illustrated here: a hemispherical dome, which has a circular base and a semicircular section; a saucer dome, which has a circular base and a segmental (less than a semicircle) section; a polyhedral dome, which is a dome on a polygonal base whose sides meet at the top of the dome; and an onion dome, which has a circular or polygonal base and an ogee-shaped section. Many domes have a lantern (a turret with windows) to provide light inside.

LANTERN AND UPPER DOME TIMBERING, ST. PAUL'S CATHEDRAL

DOME TIMBERING, CHURCH OF THE SORBONNE, PARIS, FRANCE, 1635-1642 (BY J. LEMERCIER)

Ogee-curved dome
Straight brace
Window zone
Deeply projecting pier buttress
Cornice
Depressed hood mold
Pedestal
Circular lucarne window
Floorboard
Floor joist
Ashlar piece
Hood mold
Pin
Waisted-oval lucarne window
Short strut
Mortise and tenon joint
Ogee-curved window frame
Principal rafter
Straight brace
Vertical post
Tie beam
Circular baseplate
Common rafter
Shaft connecting lantern and church interior

ROOF WITH LANTERN AND ONION DOME

Weathercock
Ellipsoid orb
Onion dome
Keeled lesene
Fish-scale tile
Octahedral base
Oversailing fascia
Sloping roof
Round arch
Tetrahedral capital
Attached pillar
Return
Vertical band
Window
Oversailing fascia
Torus
Octahedral base of lantern
Fillet
Lantern
Tetrahedral roof

REPRESENTATION OF DOME METALING, CHURCH OF THE SORBONNE

Cross
Orb
Square rib
Inverted ovolo (quarter-round)
Astragal
Volute
Fillet
Roll molding
Plain fascia
Buttress
Lantern
Round-arched window
Volute
Ovolo (quarter-round)
Cornice
Fillet
Projecting pier buttress
Dome on a circular base
Fish-scale tile
Inverted demi-heart torus molding
Hood mold
Waisted-oval lucarne window
Small volute
Gutter
Parapet
Semicircular torus molding
Small roll
Fillet
Plain fascia
Triple lesene

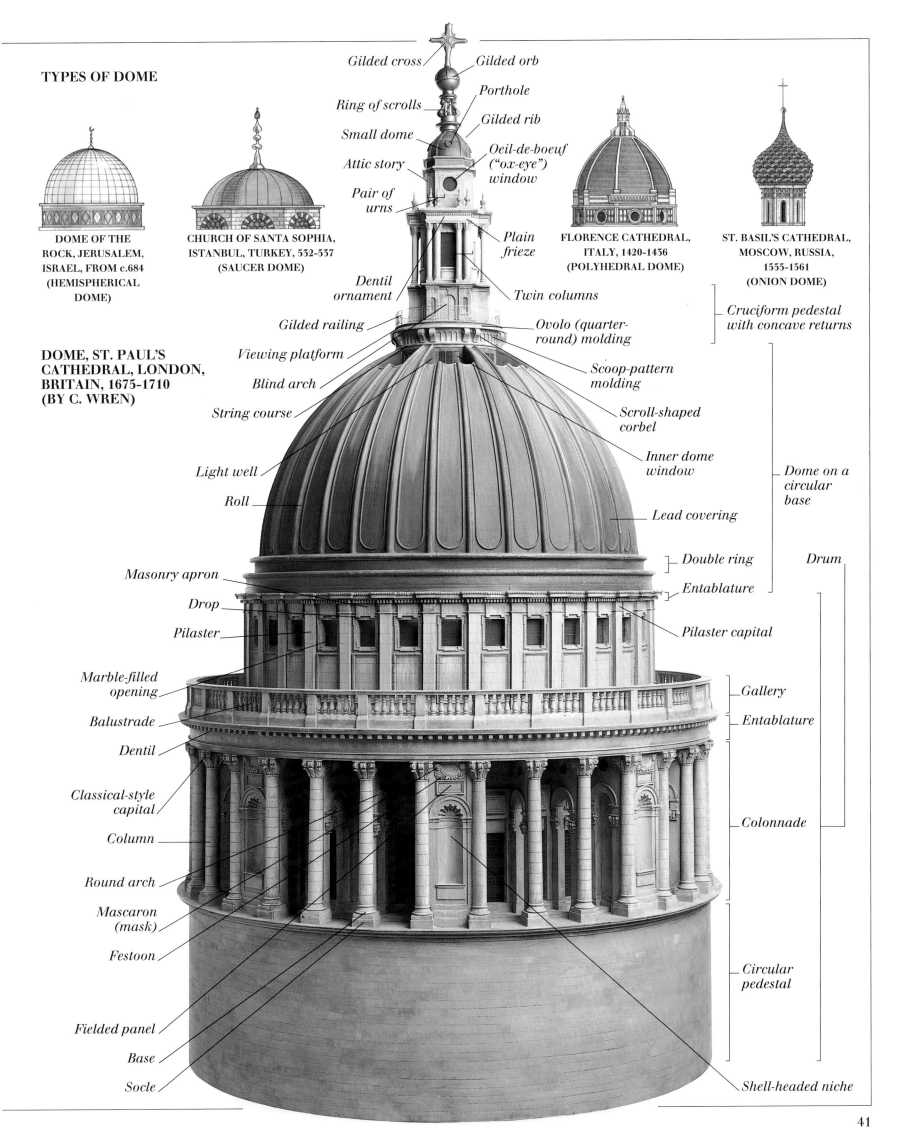

TYPES OF DOME

DOME OF THE ROCK, JERUSALEM, ISRAEL, FROM c.684 (HEMISPHERICAL DOME)

CHURCH OF SANTA SOPHIA, ISTANBUL, TURKEY, 532-537 (SAUCER DOME)

FLORENCE CATHEDRAL, ITALY, 1420-1436 (POLYHEDRAL DOME)

ST. BASIL'S CATHEDRAL, MOSCOW, RUSSIA, 1555-1561 (ONION DOME)

DOME, ST. PAUL'S CATHEDRAL, LONDON, BRITAIN, 1675-1710 (BY C. WREN)

Gilded cross

Gilded orb

Ring of scrolls

Porthole

Small dome

Gilded rib

Attic story

Oeil-de-boeuf ("ox-eye") window

Pair of urns

Plain frieze

Dentil ornament

Twin columns

Gilded railing

Ovolo (quarter-round) molding

Viewing platform

Scoop-pattern molding

Blind arch

Scroll-shaped corbel

String course

Inner dome window

Light well

Lead covering

Roll

Cruciform pedestal with concave returns

Dome on a circular base

Double ring

Drum

Masonry apron

Entablature

Drop

Pilaster capital

Pilaster

Marble-filled opening

Gallery

Balustrade

Entablature

Dentil

Classical-style capital

Colonnade

Column

Round arch

Mascaron (mask)

Festoon

Circular pedestal

Fielded panel

Base

Socle

Shell-headed niche

41

Islamic buildings

![OPUS SECTILE MOSAIC DESIGN]

OPUS SECTILE MOSAIC DESIGN

THE ISLAMIC RELIGION was founded by the prophet Mohammed, who was born in Mecca (in present-day Saudi Arabia) about 570 AD. During the next three centuries, Islam spread from Arabia to North Africa and Spain, as well as into India and much of the rest of Asia. The worldwide influence of Islam remains strong today. Common characteristics of Islamic buildings include ogee arches and roofs, onion domes, and walls decorated with carved stone, paintings, inlays, or mosaics. The most important type of Islamic building is the mosque—the place of worship—which generally has a minaret (tower) from which the muezzin (official crier) calls Muslims to prayer. Most mosques have a mihrab (decorative niche) that indicates the direction of Mecca. As figurative art is not allowed in Islam, buildings are ornamented with geometric and arabesque motifs and inscriptions (frequently Koranic verses).

Budlike onion dome
Depressed arch surrounding mihrab
Painted roof pavilion
Turkish crescent finial
Lotus flower pendentive
Crest
Arabic inscription
Painted minaret with censer (incense burner)
Spandrel
Series of recessed arches
Semidome
Arched niche within a niche
Mural resembling tomb
Polyhedral niche
Recessed colonettes

MIHRAB, JAMI MASJID (PRINCIPAL OR CONGREGATIONAL MOSQUE), BIJAPUR, INDIA, c.1636

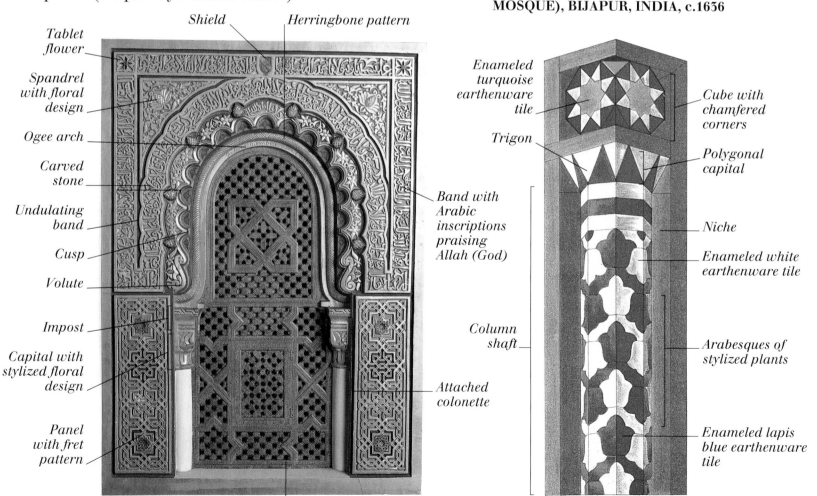

Tablet flower
Shield
Herringbone pattern
Spandrel with floral design
Ogee arch
Carved stone
Undulating band
Cusp
Volute
Impost
Capital with stylized floral design
Panel with fret pattern
Band with Arabic inscriptions praising Allah (God)
Attached colonette

Jali (latticed screen) with geometrical patterns

ARCH, THE ALHAMBRA, GRANADA, SPAIN, 1333-1354

Enameled turquoise earthenware tile
Trigon
Column shaft
Cube with chamfered corners
Polygonal capital
Niche
Enameled white earthenware tile
Arabesques of stylized plants
Enameled lapis blue earthenware tile

MIHRAB WITH COLUMN, EL-AINYI MOSQUE, CAIRO, EGYPT, 15TH CENTURY

EXAMPLES OF ISLAMIC MOSAICS, EGYPT AND SYRIA

Star-shaped motif

Triangle of yellow marble

Greek cross of red marble

Rhombus of black marble

Stone band

STAR AND GREEK CROSS MOSAIC

Stone

Black marble

Mosaic tessellation

Turquoise glass

Tessera (small mosaic piece)

FRET-PATTERN MOSAIC

Greek cross of black and yellow marble

Star-shaped motif

Stone band

Rhombus of red marble

STAR AND GREEK CROSS MOSAIC

Parallelogram of black marble

Symmetrical quadrilateral of stone

Triangle of yellow marble

Rhombus of red marble

Star-shaped motif

MOSAIC OF HEXAGONS, TRIANGLES, AND SYMMETRICAL QUADRILATERALS

Hexagonal design

Band of black marble

Band of stone

HEXAGON AND BAND MOSAIC

Triangle of turquoise glass

Parallelogram of mother-of-pearl

DANCETTE (ZIG-ZAG)-PATTERN MOSAIC

Symmetrical quadrilateral of black marble

Hexagon of red marble

Triangle of stone

MOSAIC OF HEXAGONS, TRIANGLES, AND SYMMETRICAL QUADRILATERALS

MARBLE TOMB OF ITIMAD-UD-DAULA, AGRA, INDIA, c.1622-1628

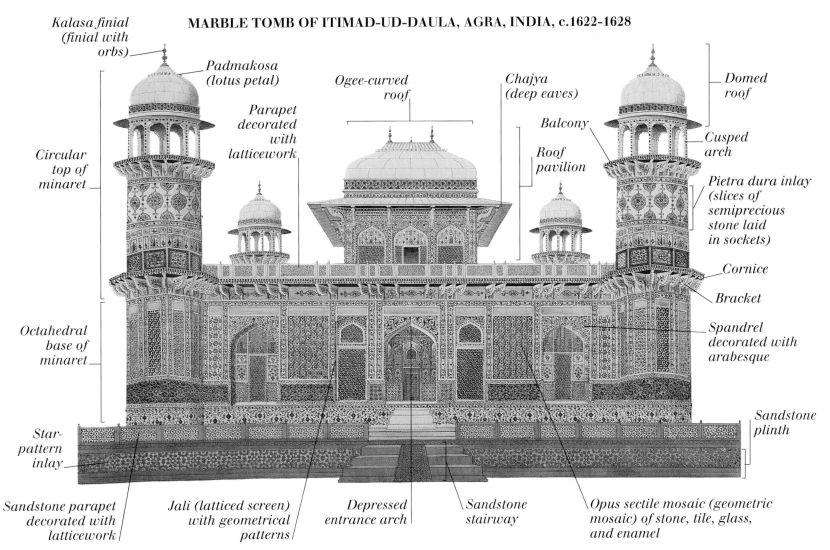

Kalasa finial (finial with orbs)

Padmakosa (lotus petal)

Ogee-curved roof

Chajya (deep eaves)

Domed roof

Circular top of minaret

Parapet decorated with latticework

Balcony

Cusped arch

Roof pavilion

Pietra dura inlay (slices of semiprecious stone laid in sockets)

Cornice

Bracket

Octahedral base of minaret

Spandrel decorated with arabesque

Star-pattern inlay

Sandstone plinth

Sandstone parapet decorated with latticework

Jali (latticed screen) with geometrical patterns

Depressed entrance arch

Sandstone stairway

Opus sectile mosaic (geometric mosaic) of stone, tile, glass, and enamel

43

South and east Asia

THE TRADITIONAL ARCHITECTURE of south and east Asia has been profoundly influenced by the spread from India of Buddhism and Hinduism. This influence is shown by both the abundance and by the architectural styles of temples and shrines in the region. Many early Hindu temples consist of rooms carved from solid rock faces. However, freestanding structures began to be built in southern India from about the eighth century AD. Many were built in the Dravidian style, like the Temple of Virupaksha (opposite), with its characteristic antarala (terraced tower), perforated windows, and numerous arches, pilasters, and carvings. The earliest Buddhist religious monuments were Indian stupas (see pp. 58-59), which consisted of a single hemispherical dome surmounted by a chattravali (shaft) and surrounded by railings with ornate gates. Later Indian stupas and those built elsewhere were sometimes modified. For example, in Sri Lanka, the dome became bell-shaped, and was called a dagoba. Buddhist pagodas, such as the Burmese example (right), are multistoried temples, each story having a projecting roof. The form of these buildings probably derived from the yasti (pointed spire) of the stupa. Another feature of many traditional Asian buildings is their imaginative roof forms, such as gambrel (mansard) roofs, and roofs with angle rafters (below).

DETAILS FROM EAST ASIAN BUILDINGS

KASUGA-STYLE ROOF WITH SUMIGI (ANGLE RAFTERS), KASUGADO SHRINE OF ENJOJI, NARA, JAPAN, 12TH-14TH CENTURY

TERRACES, TEMPLE OF HEAVEN, BEIJING, CHINA, 15TH CENTURY

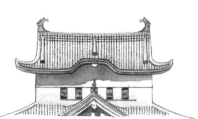

GAMBREL (MANSARD) ROOF WITH UPSWEPT EAVES AND UNDULATING GABLES, HIMEJI CASTLE, HIMEJI, JAPAN, 1608-1609

CORNER CAPITAL WITH ROOF BEAMS, POPCHU-SA TEMPLE, POPCHU-SA, SOUTH KOREA, 17TH CENTURY

SEVEN-STORIED PAGODA IN BURMESE STYLE, c.9TH-10TH CENTURY

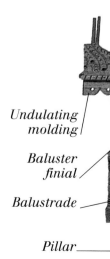

Gilded band

Gilded iron hti (crown)

Dubika (mast)

Arrow motif

Torus molding with spiral carving

Decorative eaves board

Ogee-arched motif with decorative carvings

Ogee-arched motif forming horn

Hip rafter

Pentroof

Undulating molding

Engaged pillar

Arched entrance

Baluster finial

Rectangular window

Balustrade

Baluster

Pillar

Straight brace

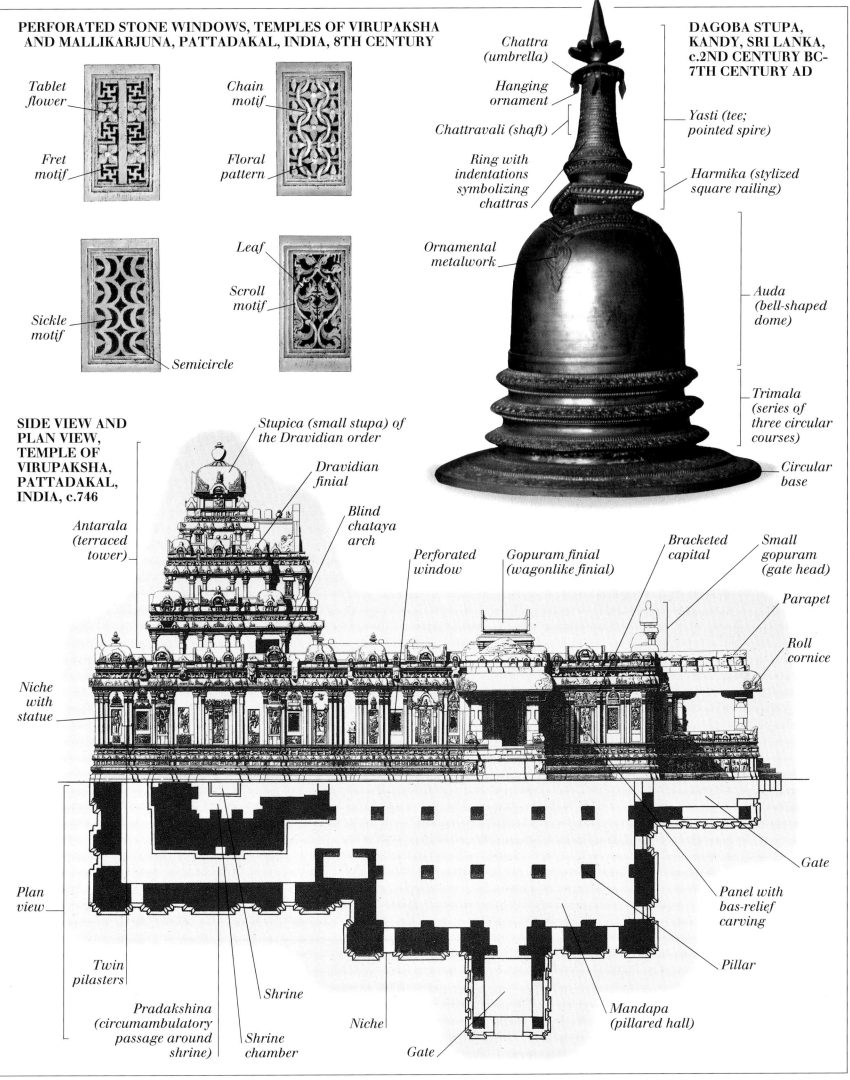

PERFORATED STONE WINDOWS, TEMPLES OF VIRUPAKSHA AND MALLIKARJUNA, PATTADAKAL, INDIA, 8TH CENTURY

Tablet flower

Chain motif

Fret motif

Floral pattern

Leaf

Scroll motif

Sickle motif

Semicircle

DAGOBA STUPA, KANDY, SRI LANKA, c.2ND CENTURY BC-7TH CENTURY AD

Chattra (umbrella)

Hanging ornament

Chattravali (shaft)

Ring with indentations symbolizing chattras

Ornamental metalwork

Yasti (tee; pointed spire)

Harmika (stylized square railing)

Auda (bell-shaped dome)

Trimala (series of three circular courses)

Circular base

SIDE VIEW AND PLAN VIEW, TEMPLE OF VIRUPAKSHA, PATTADAKAL, INDIA, c.746

Stupica (small stupa) of the Dravidian order

Dravidian finial

Blind chataya arch

Antarala (terraced tower)

Perforated window

Gopuram finial (wagonlike finial)

Bracketed capital

Small gopuram (gate head)

Parapet

Roll cornice

Niche with statue

Gate

Panel with bas-relief carving

Plan view

Pillar

Twin pilasters

Shrine

Pradakshina (circumambulatory passage around shrine)

Shrine chamber

Niche

Gate

Mandapa (pillared hall)

45

Doors

A DOOR AND ITS SURROUNDING FRAME make up a doorway. Doorways that are particularly grand or imposing are known as portals, examples of which include the portals of Lund and Cologne cathedrals (opposite). There are two main types of door, paneled and matchboarded, both of which were used as long ago as ancient Egyptian times. Paneled doors consist of a frame of horizontal rails and vertical muntins, with infilled panels of wood or glass. Matchboarded doors consist of long vertical boards held in position by horizontal rails and diagonal braces.

PANELED DOOR

Top rail

Arch

Glazed panel

Muntin

Mail slot

Bolection molding

Panel

Bottom rail

PARTS OF A PANELED DOOR

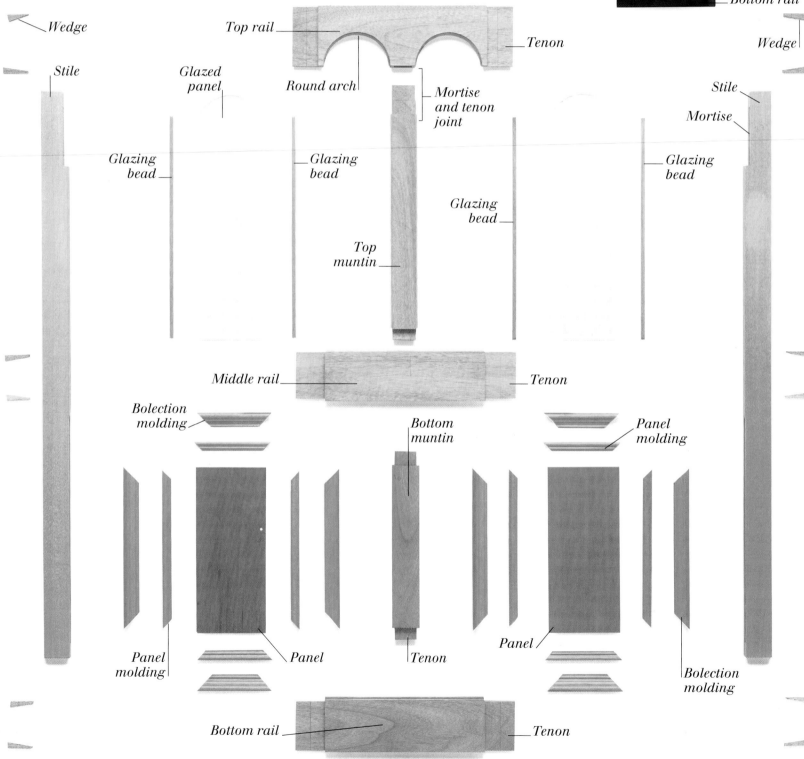

Wedge

Stile

Glazed panel

Top rail

Tenon

Wedge

Stile

Round arch

Mortise and tenon joint

Mortise

Glazing bead

Glazing bead

Glazing bead

Glazing bead

Glazing bead

Top muntin

Middle rail

Tenon

Bolection molding

Bottom muntin

Panel molding

Panel molding

Panel

Tenon

Panel

Panel molding

Panel

Tenon

Bolection molding

Bottom rail

Tenon

TYPES OF DOOR

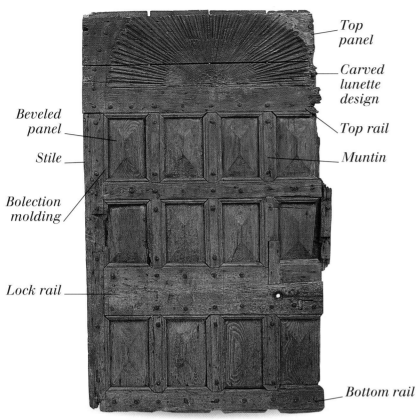

Top panel

Carved lunette design

Top rail

Muntin

Beveled panel

Stile

Bolection molding

Lock rail

Bottom rail

PANELED EXTERNAL DOOR, HOUSE, SURREY, BRITAIN, c.1625-1630

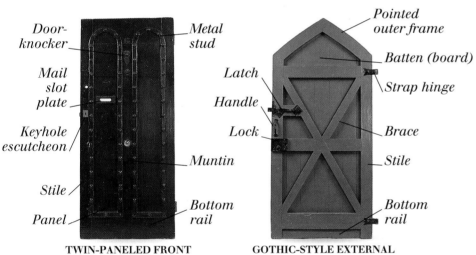

Door-knocker

Metal stud

Mail slot plate

Keyhole escutcheon

Muntin

Stile

Panel

Bottom rail

Pointed outer frame

Batten (board)

Latch

Strap hinge

Handle

Lock

Brace

Stile

Bottom rail

TWIN-PANELED FRONT DOOR, HOUSE, LONDON, BRITAIN, c.1830

GOTHIC-STYLE EXTERNAL MATCHBOARDED DOOR, RIPLEY CHURCH SCHOOL, BRITAIN, c.1846

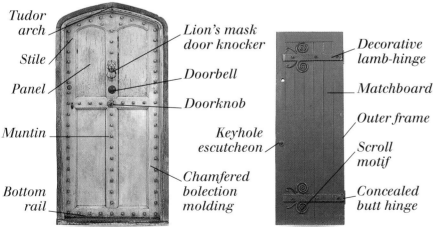

Tudor arch

Stile

Panel

Muntin

Bottom rail

Lion's mask door knocker

Doorbell

Doorknob

Keyhole escutcheon

Chamfered bolection molding

Decorative lamb-hinge

Matchboard

Outer frame

Scroll motif

Concealed butt hinge

TUDOR-STYLE FOUR-PANELED FRONT DOOR, VILLA, GODALMING, BRITAIN, c.1859

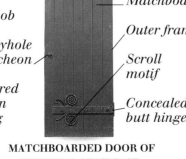

MATCHBOARDED DOOR OF INTERNAL STAIRCASE, RAINHILL ASYLUM, BRITAIN, c.1884

TYPES OF DOORWAY AND PORTAL

THE GATE OF THE SUN, TIAHUANACO, BOLIVIA, c.600-1000

ANGLO-SAXON TRIANGULAR-ARCHED DOORWAY, BRITAIN, c.900

IONIC DOORWAY, THE ERECHTHEION, ATHENS, GREECE, 421-405 BC

ROMANESQUE PORTAL, LUND CATHEDRAL, SWEDEN, FROM c.1103

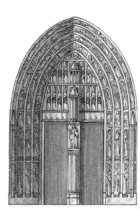

GOTHIC PORTAL, COLOGNE CATHEDRAL, GERMANY, FROM 1248

RENAISSANCE DOORWAY, CHURCH OF ST. ZACCARIA, VENICE, ITALY, FROM 1483

ART NOUVEAU ELLIPSOID DOORWAY, PALAU GÜELL, BARCELONA, SPAIN, 1885-1889

ART DECO ELEVATOR DOORS, CHRYSLER BUILDING, NEW YORK, USA, 1928-1930

Windows

OEIL-DE-BOEUF ("OX-EYE") WINDOW

THE EARLIEST windows were simply openings for light and ventilation. Glazed windows were first used by the ancient Romans, but they did not appear often in domestic houses until the 16th century. Early glazing consisted of quarrels (small panes of glass) held together by cames (lead strips) to form a light. As windows became larger, the individual lights were joined together by horizontal transoms and vertical mullions. Casement windows and sash windows originated in the 16th and 17th centuries. A casement window can be swung open on a hinge attached to the side of the window frame, whereas a sash window slides up and down on a sash cord attached, by a pulley, to a weight. The development of metal frames—as in the Bauhaus windows at Dessau, Germany—and the availability of large panes of glass eventually made it possible to cover buildings almost entirely with glass.

SECTION FROM STEEL CASEMENT WINDOW, 1907

Top rail
Top bolt
Socket
Bolt operated by casement handle
Latch
Decorative handle-plate
Casement handle
Iron shaft
Stile

FANLIGHT, c.1700

Rosette motif
Lead tracery bar
Pane
Outer timber frame
Glazing bar
Bottom rail

CASEMENT WINDOW, c.1925

Head
Horn
Quarrel
Stile
Casement fastener
Cockspur-pattern handle
Chamfered molding
Window frame
Bottom rail
Oak sill
Casement stay
Window sash
Lead came
Post

STAINED GLASS (DETAILS) FROM THE ROYAL COURTS OF JUSTICE, LONDON, BRITAIN, 1866

Coat of arms
Lead came
Quarrel
Circular quarrel
Diaper work (background design)
Rectangular quarrel

VICTORIAN WINDOW WITH SEGMENTAL HEAD, c.1899

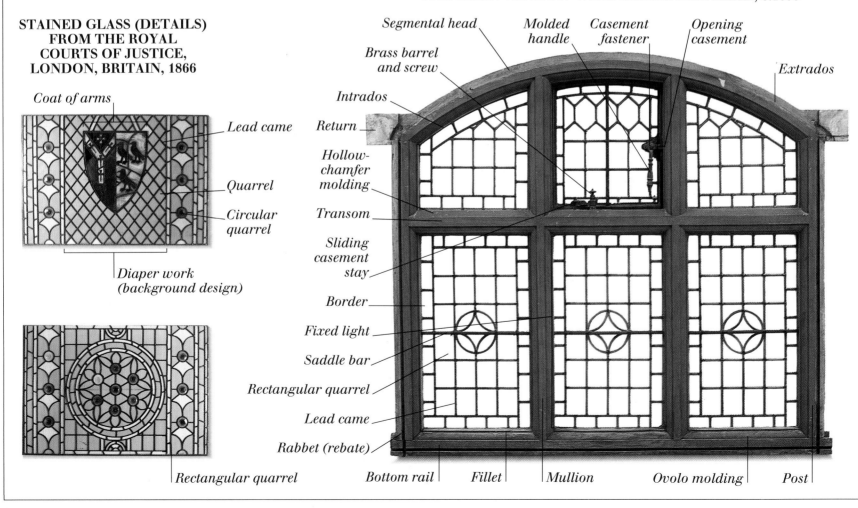

Segmental head
Molded handle
Casement fastener
Opening casement
Brass barrel and screw
Intrados
Return
Hollow-chamfer molding
Transom
Sliding casement stay
Border
Fixed light
Saddle bar
Rectangular quarrel
Lead came
Rabbet (rebate)
Extrados
Bottom rail
Fillet
Mullion
Ovolo molding
Post

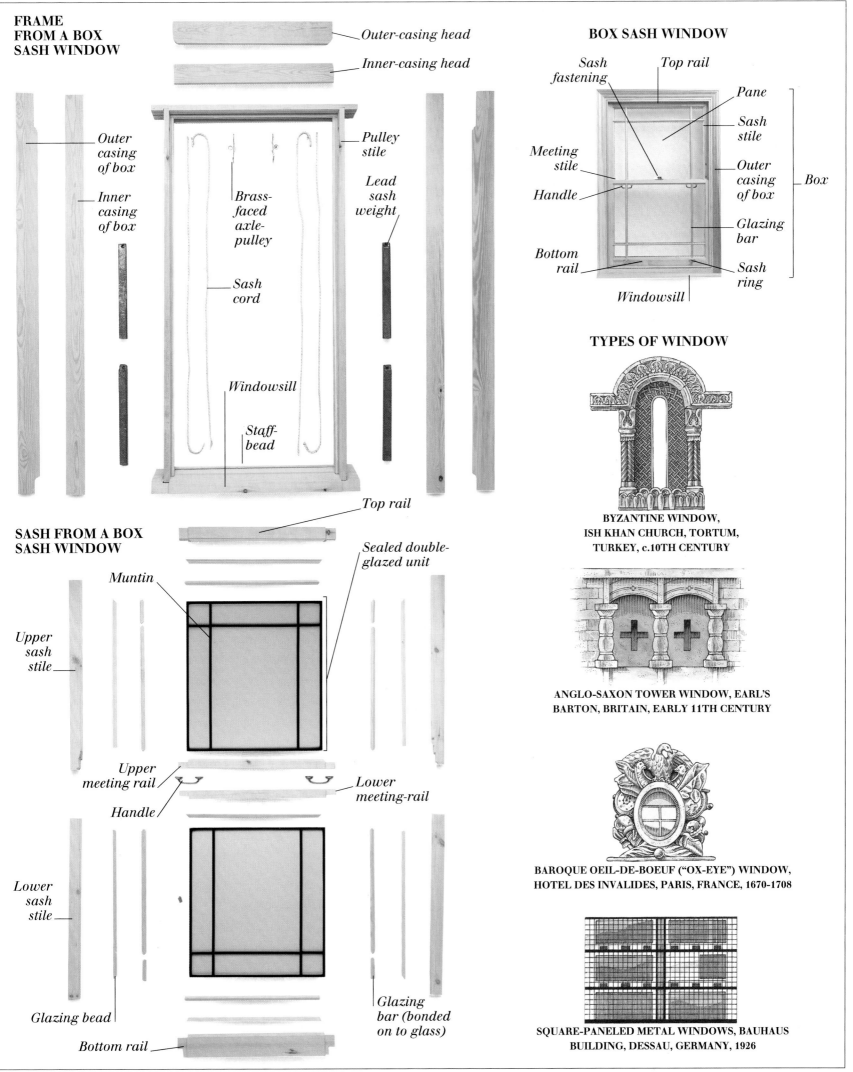

FRAME FROM A BOX SASH WINDOW

Outer-casing head

Inner-casing head

Outer casing of box

Inner casing of box

Brass-faced axle-pulley

Sash cord

Windowsill

Staff-bead

Pulley stile

Lead sash weight

BOX SASH WINDOW

Sash fastening

Top rail

Pane

Sash stile

Meeting stile

Handle

Outer casing of box

Box

Bottom rail

Glazing bar

Sash ring

Windowsill

TYPES OF WINDOW

BYZANTINE WINDOW, ISH KHAN CHURCH, TORTUM, TURKEY, c.10TH CENTURY

ANGLO-SAXON TOWER WINDOW, EARL'S BARTON, BRITAIN, EARLY 11TH CENTURY

BAROQUE OEIL-DE-BOEUF ("OX-EYE") WINDOW, HOTEL DES INVALIDES, PARIS, FRANCE, 1670-1708

SQUARE-PANELED METAL WINDOWS, BAUHAUS BUILDING, DESSAU, GERMANY, 1926

SASH FROM A BOX SASH WINDOW

Top rail

Sealed double-glazed unit

Muntin

Upper sash stile

Upper meeting rail

Handle

Lower meeting-rail

Lower sash stile

Glazing bead

Glazing bar (bonded on to glass)

Bottom rail

The 19th century

BUILDINGS OF THE 19TH CENTURY are characterized by the use of new materials and by a great diversity of architectural styles. From the end of the 18th century, iron and steel became widely used as an alternative to wood for the framework of buildings, as in the flax-spinning mill shown here. Built in Britain in 1796, this mill exemplifies an architectural style that became common throughout the industrialized world for more than a century. The Industrial Revolution also brought mass production of building parts—a development that enabled the British architect Sir Joseph Paxton to erect London's Crystal Palace (a building made entirely of iron and glass) in only nine months, ready for the Great Exhibition of 1851. The 19th century saw a widespread revival of older architectural styles. For example, in the United States and Germany, Neo-Greek architecture was fashionable; in Britain and France, Neo-Baroque, Neo-Byzantine, and Neo-Gothic styles (as seen in the Palace of Westminster and Tower Bridge, London) were dominant.

**FLAX-SPINNING MILL,
SHREWSBURY, BRITAIN,
1796 (BY C. BAGE)**

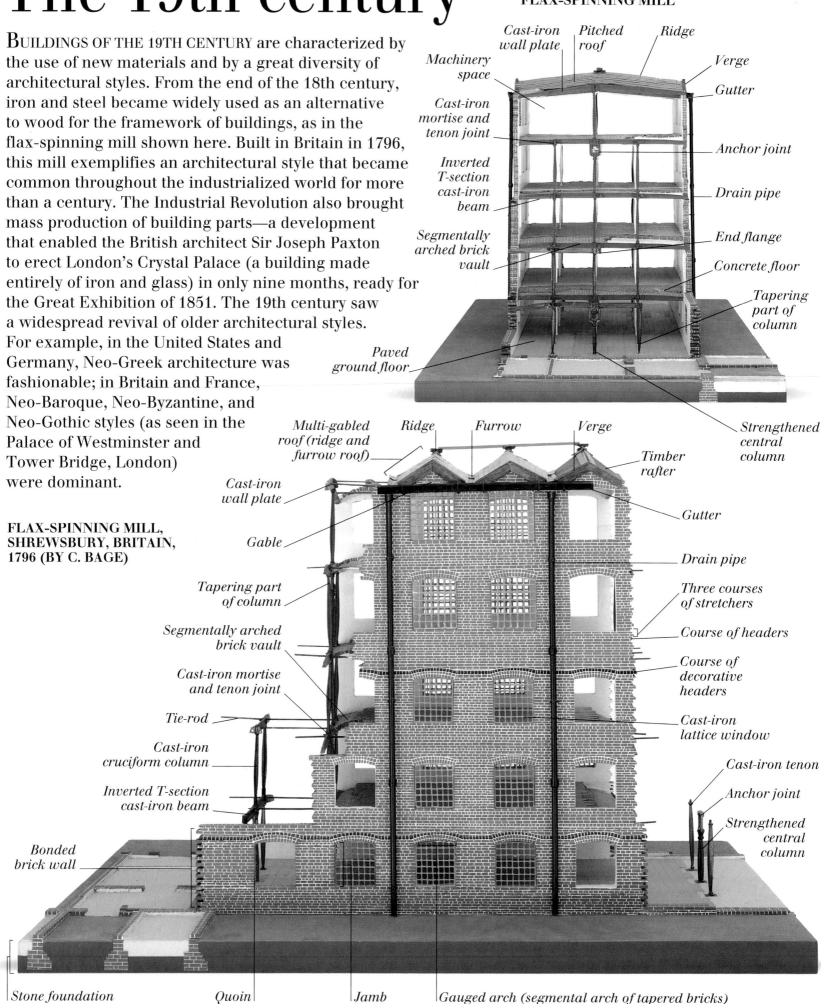

Cast-iron wall plate
Pitched roof
Ridge
Machinery space
Verge
Gutter
Cast-iron mortise and tenon joint
Anchor joint
Inverted T-section cast-iron beam
Drain pipe
Segmentally arched brick vault
End flange
Concrete floor
Tapering part of column
Paved ground floor
Strengthened central column

Multi-gabled roof (ridge and furrow roof)
Ridge
Furrow
Verge
Timber rafter
Cast-iron wall plate
Gutter
Gable
Drain pipe
Tapering part of column
Three courses of stretchers
Segmentally arched brick vault
Course of headers
Cast-iron mortise and tenon joint
Course of decorative headers
Tie-rod
Cast-iron cruciform column
Cast-iron lattice window
Inverted T-section cast-iron beam
Cast-iron tenon
Anchor joint
Strengthened central column
Bonded brick wall

Stone foundation
Quoin
Jamb
Gauged arch (segmental arch of tapered bricks)

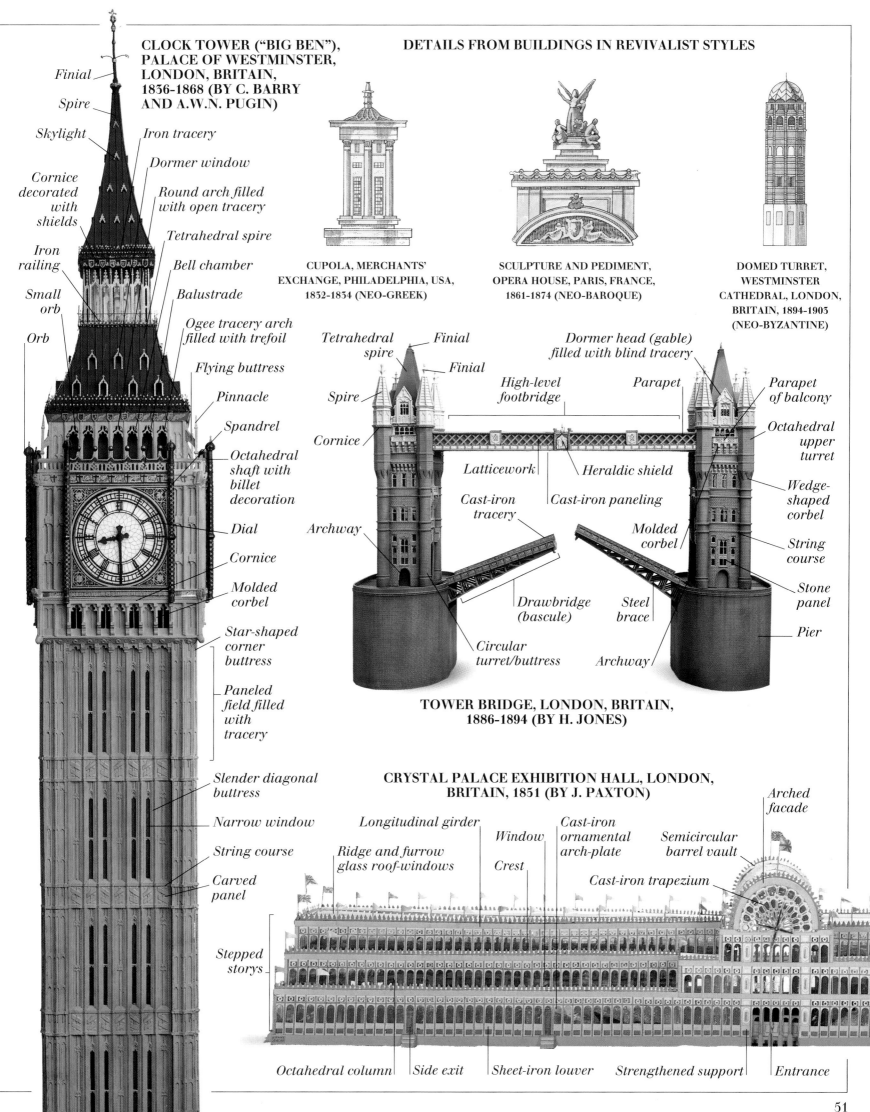

CLOCK TOWER ("BIG BEN"), PALACE OF WESTMINSTER, LONDON, BRITAIN, 1836-1868 (BY C. BARRY AND A.W.N. PUGIN)

Finial

Spire

Skylight

Iron tracery

Cornice decorated with shields

Dormer window

Round arch filled with open tracery

Tetrahedral spire

Iron railing

Bell chamber

Small orb

Balustrade

Orb

Ogee tracery arch filled with trefoil

Flying buttress

Pinnacle

Spandrel

Octahedral shaft with billet decoration

Dial

Cornice

Molded corbel

Star-shaped corner buttress

Paneled field filled with tracery

Slender diagonal buttress

Narrow window

String course

Carved panel

DETAILS FROM BUILDINGS IN REVIVALIST STYLES

CUPOLA, MERCHANTS' EXCHANGE, PHILADELPHIA, USA, 1832-1834 (NEO-GREEK)

SCULPTURE AND PEDIMENT, OPERA HOUSE, PARIS, FRANCE, 1861-1874 (NEO-BAROQUE)

DOMED TURRET, WESTMINSTER CATHEDRAL, LONDON, BRITAIN, 1894-1903 (NEO-BYZANTINE)

Tetrahedral spire

Finial

Finial

Spire

Cornice

High-level footbridge

Dormer head (gable) filled with blind tracery

Parapet

Parapet of balcony

Octahedral upper turret

Latticework

Heraldic shield

Cast-iron tracery

Cast-iron paneling

Wedge-shaped corbel

Archway

Molded corbel

String course

Drawbridge (bascule)

Steel brace

Stone panel

Circular turret/buttress

Archway

Pier

TOWER BRIDGE, LONDON, BRITAIN, 1886-1894 (BY H. JONES)

CRYSTAL PALACE EXHIBITION HALL, LONDON, BRITAIN, 1851 (BY J. PAXTON)

Arched facade

Longitudinal girder

Cast-iron ornamental arch-plate

Window

Semicircular barrel vault

Ridge and furrow glass roof-windows

Crest

Cast-iron trapezium

Stepped storys

Octahedral column

Side exit

Sheet-iron louver

Strengthened support

Entrance

The early 20th century

ARCHITECTURE OF THE EARLY 20TH CENTURY is notable for radical new types of steel and glass buildings—particularly skyscrapers—and the widespread use of steel-reinforced concrete. The steel-framed skyscraper was pioneered in Chicago in the 1880s but did not become widespread until the first decades of the 20th century. As construction techniques were refined, skyscrapers became higher and higher. For example, the Empire State Building (right) of 1929-1931 has 102 storys. Many buildings of this period were constructed from lightweight concrete slabs that could be supported by cantilever beams or by pilotis (stilts), as in the Villa Savoye (below). The early 20th century also produced a great variety of architectural styles, some of which are illustrated opposite. Despite their diversity, the styles of this period generally had one thing in common: they were completely new, with few links to past architectural styles. This originality is in marked contrast to 19th-century architecture (see pp. 50-51), much of which was revivalist.

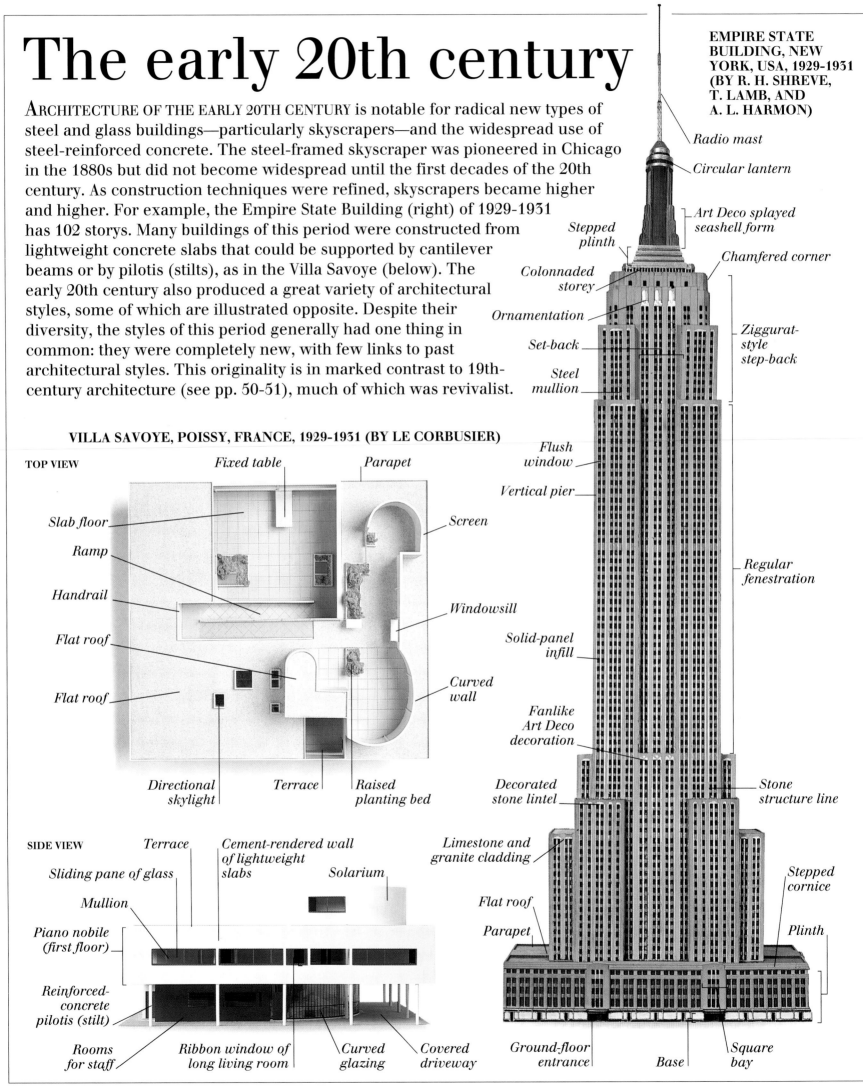

EMPIRE STATE BUILDING, NEW YORK, USA, 1929-1931 (BY R. H. SHREVE, T. LAMB, AND A. L. HARMON)

- Radio mast
- Circular lantern
- Art Deco splayed seashell form
- Stepped plinth
- Chamfered corner
- Colonnaded storey
- Ornamentation
- Ziggurat-style step-back
- Set-back
- Steel mullion
- Flush window
- Vertical pier
- Regular fenestration
- Solid-panel infill
- Fanlike Art Deco decoration
- Decorated stone lintel
- Stone structure line
- Limestone and granite cladding
- Stepped cornice
- Flat roof
- Plinth
- Parapet
- Ground-floor entrance
- Base
- Square bay

VILLA SAVOYE, POISSY, FRANCE, 1929-1931 (BY LE CORBUSIER)

TOP VIEW

- Fixed table
- Parapet
- Slab floor
- Screen
- Ramp
- Handrail
- Windowsill
- Flat roof
- Curved wall
- Flat roof
- Directional skylight
- Terrace
- Raised planting bed

SIDE VIEW

- Terrace
- Cement-rendered wall of lightweight slabs
- Solarium
- Sliding pane of glass
- Mullion
- Piano nobile (first floor)
- Reinforced-concrete pilotis (stilt)
- Rooms for staff
- Ribbon window of long living room
- Curved glazing
- Covered driveway

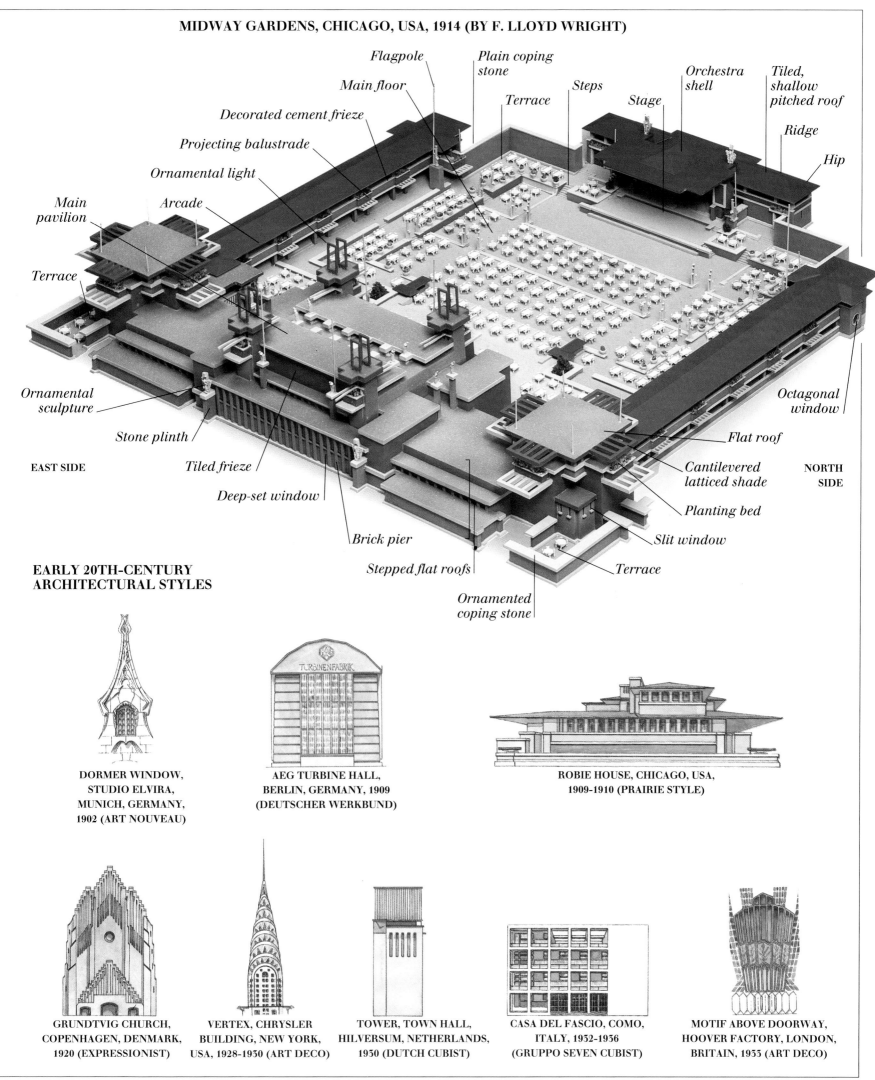

MIDWAY GARDENS, CHICAGO, USA, 1914 (BY F. LLOYD WRIGHT)

Flagpole

Plain coping stone

Main floor

Orchestra shell

Tiled, shallow pitched roof

Decorated cement frieze

Terrace

Steps

Stage

Ridge

Projecting balustrade

Hip

Ornamental light

Main pavilion

Arcade

Terrace

Octagonal window

Ornamental sculpture

EAST SIDE

Stone plinth

Tiled frieze

Flat roof

NORTH SIDE

Deep-set window

Cantilevered latticed shade

Brick pier

Planting bed

Slit window

Stepped flat roofs

Terrace

EARLY 20TH-CENTURY ARCHITECTURAL STYLES

Ornamented coping stone

DORMER WINDOW, STUDIO ELVIRA, MUNICH, GERMANY, 1902 (ART NOUVEAU)

AEG TURBINE HALL, BERLIN, GERMANY, 1909 (DEUTSCHER WERKBUND)

ROBIE HOUSE, CHICAGO, USA, 1909-1910 (PRAIRIE STYLE)

GRUNDTVIG CHURCH, COPENHAGEN, DENMARK, 1920 (EXPRESSIONIST)

VERTEX, CHRYSLER BUILDING, NEW YORK, USA, 1928-1930 (ART DECO)

TOWER, TOWN HALL, HILVERSUM, NETHERLANDS, 1930 (DUTCH CUBIST)

CASA DEL FASCIO, COMO, ITALY, 1932-1936 (GRUPPO SEVEN CUBIST)

MOTIF ABOVE DOORWAY, HOOVER FACTORY, LONDON, BRITAIN, 1933 (ART DECO)

Modern buildings 1

ARCHITECTURE SINCE ABOUT THE 1950s is generally known as modern architecture. One of its main influences has been functionalism—a belief that a building's function should be apparent in its design. Both the Centre Georges Pompidou (below and opposite) and the Hong Kong and Shanghai Bank (see pp. 56-57) are functionalist buildings. On each, elements of engineering and the building's services are clearly visible on the outside. In the 1980s, some architects rejected functionalism in favor of postmodernism, in which historical styles—particularly neoclassicism—were revived, using modern building materials and techniques. In many modern buildings, walls are made of glass or concrete hung from a frame, as in the Kawana House (right); this type of wall construction is known as curtain walling. Other modern construction techniques include the intricate interlocking of concrete vaults—as in the Sydney Opera House (see pp. 56-57)—and the use of high-tension beams to create complex roof shapes, such as the paraboloid roof of the Church of St. Pierre de Libreville (see pp. 56-57).

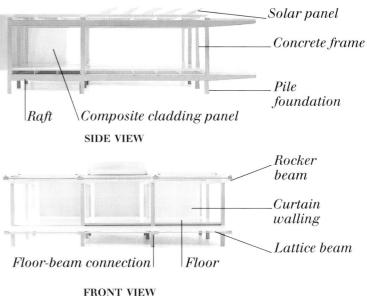

Solar panel
Concrete frame
Pile foundation
Raft *Composite cladding panel*

SIDE VIEW

Rocker beam
Curtain walling
Lattice beam
Floor-beam connection *Floor*

FRONT VIEW

SERVICES FACADE, CENTRE GEORGES POMPIDOU, PARIS, FRANCE, 1977 (BY R. PIANO AND R. ROGERS)

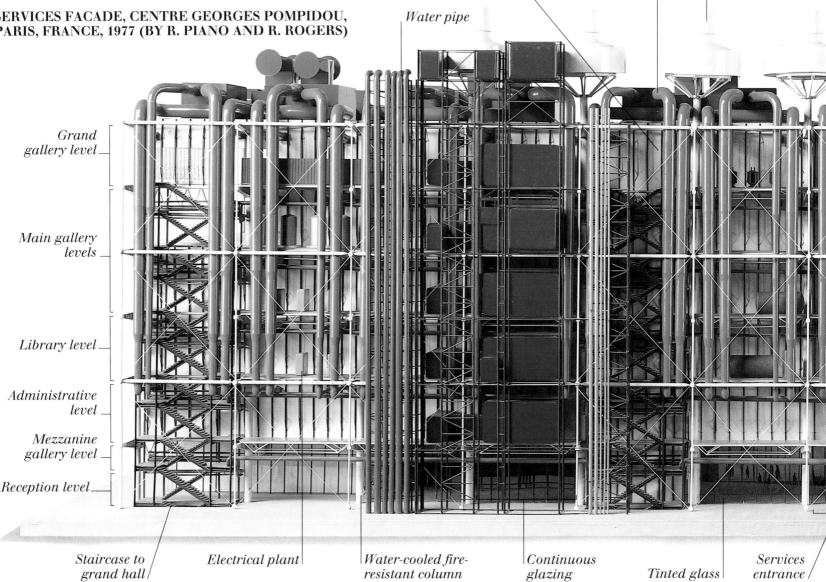

Metal-faced fire-resistant panel   *Air-conditioning duct*   *Cooling tower*

Water pipe

Grand gallery level

Main gallery levels

Library level

Administrative level

Mezzanine gallery level

Reception level

Staircase to grand hall   *Electrical plant*   *Water-cooled fire-resistant column*   *Continuous glazing*   *Tinted glass*   *Services entrance*

PRINCIPAL FACADE, CENTRE GEORGES POMPIDOU

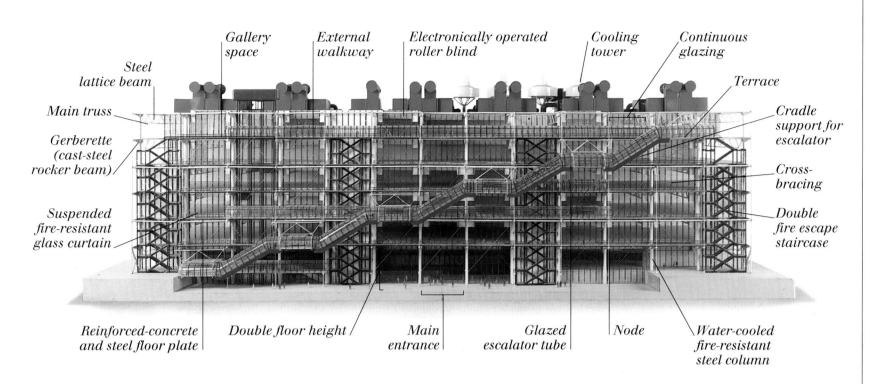

Steel lattice beam

Gallery space

External walkway

Electronically operated roller blind

Cooling tower

Continuous glazing

Main truss

Terrace

Gerberette (cast-steel rocker beam)

Cradle support for escalator

Cross-bracing

Suspended fire-resistant glass curtain

Double fire escape staircase

Reinforced-concrete and steel floor plate

Double floor height

Main entrance

Glazed escalator tube

Node

Water-cooled fire-resistant steel column

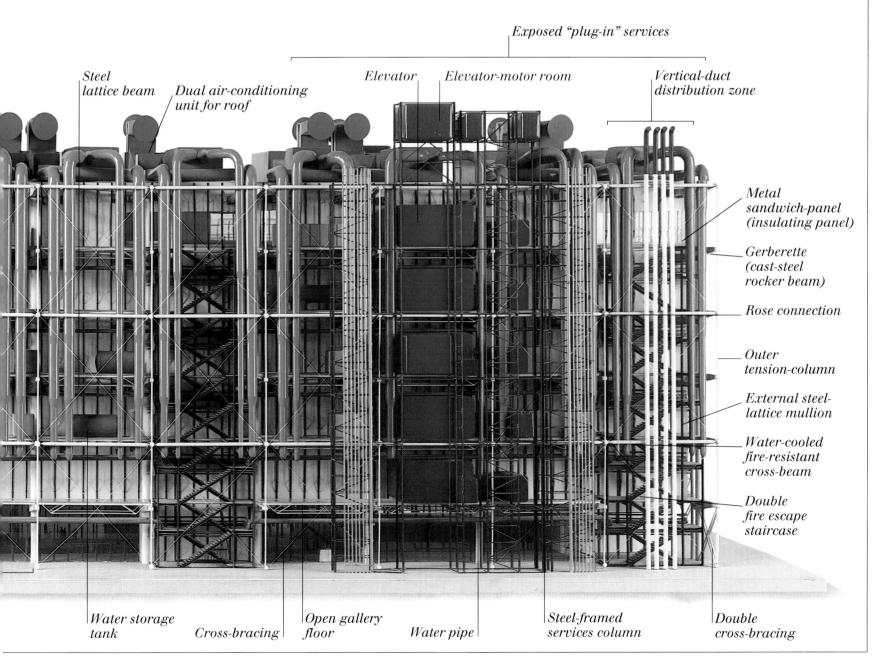

Exposed "plug-in" services

Steel lattice beam

Dual air-conditioning unit for roof

Elevator

Elevator-motor room

Vertical-duct distribution zone

Metal sandwich-panel (insulating panel)

Gerberette (cast-steel rocker beam)

Rose connection

Outer tension-column

External steel-lattice mullion

Water-cooled fire-resistant cross-beam

Double fire escape staircase

Water storage tank

Cross-bracing

Open gallery floor

Water pipe

Steel-framed services column

Double cross-bracing

Modern buildings 2

HONG KONG AND SHANGHAI BANK, HONG KONG, 1981-1985 (BY N. FOSTER)

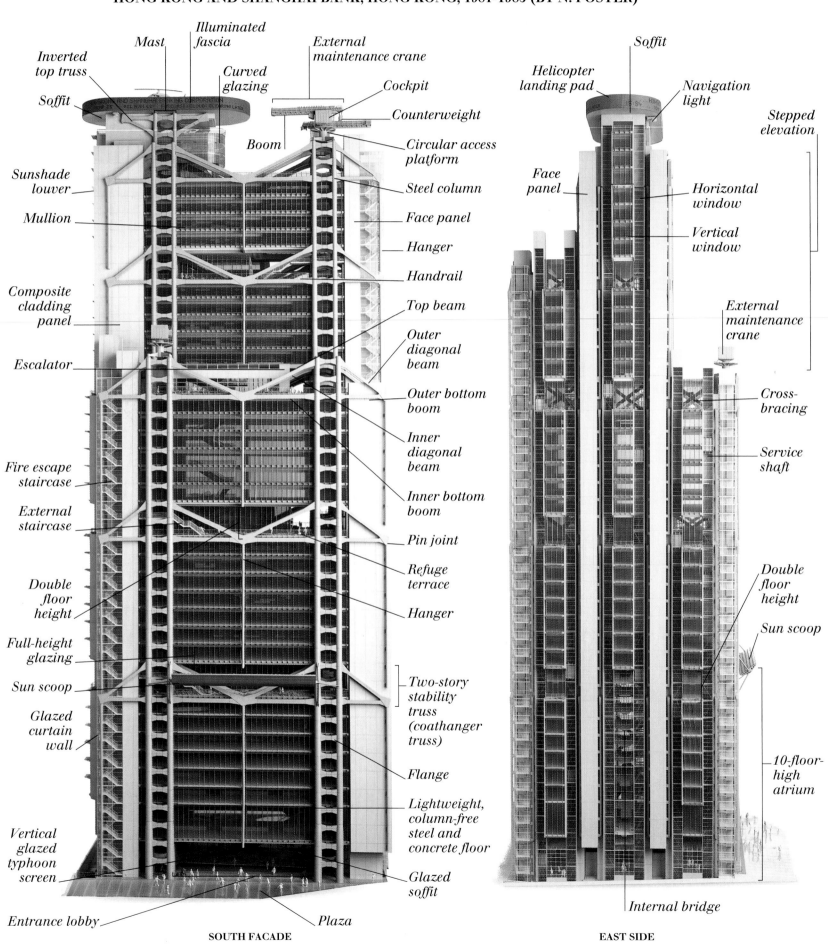

Inverted top truss

Mast

Illuminated fascia

External maintenance crane

Soffit

Soffit

Curved glazing

Cockpit

Helicopter landing pad

Navigation light

Stepped elevation

Boom

Counterweight

Sunshade louver

Circular access platform

Face panel

Horizontal window

Mullion

Steel column

Face panel

Vertical window

Hanger

Composite cladding panel

Handrail

Top beam

External maintenance crane

Escalator

Outer diagonal beam

Cross-bracing

Outer bottom boom

Service shaft

Fire escape staircase

Inner diagonal beam

External staircase

Inner bottom boom

Double floor height

Pin joint

Refuge terrace

Double floor height

Full-height glazing

Hanger

Sun scoop

Sun scoop

Glazed curtain wall

Two-story stability truss (coathanger truss)

Glazed soffit

10-floor-high atrium

Vertical glazed typhoon screen

Flange

Lightweight, column-free steel and concrete floor

Entrance lobby

Plaza

Glazed soffit

Internal bridge

SOUTH FACADE

EAST SIDE

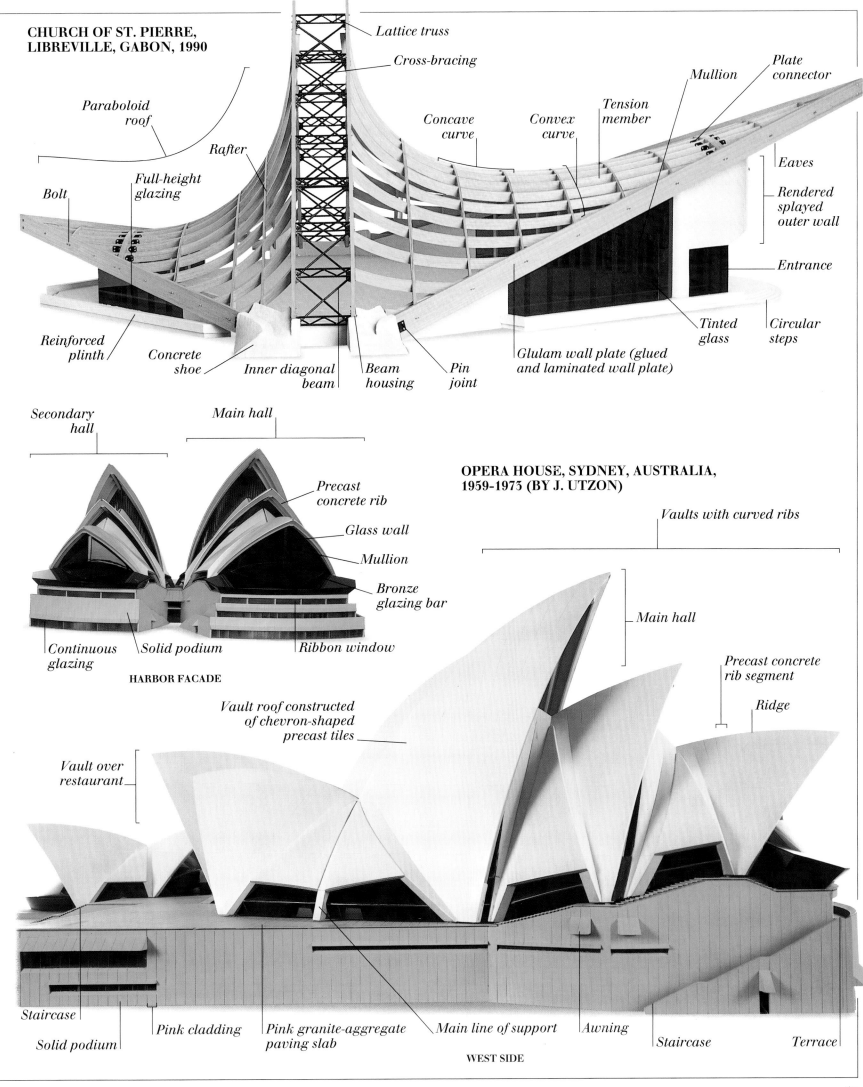

CHURCH OF ST. PIERRE, LIBREVILLE, GABON, 1990

Lattice truss

Cross-bracing

Paraboloid roof

Rafter

Concave curve

Convex curve

Tension member

Mullion

Plate connector

Bolt

Full-height glazing

Eaves

Rendered splayed outer wall

Entrance

Reinforced plinth

Concrete shoe

Inner diagonal beam

Beam housing

Pin joint

Tinted glass

Glulam wall plate (glued and laminated wall plate)

Circular steps

Secondary hall

Main hall

OPERA HOUSE, SYDNEY, AUSTRALIA, 1959-1973 (BY J. UTZON)

Precast concrete rib

Glass wall

Mullion

Bronze glazing bar

Vaults with curved ribs

Main hall

Precast concrete rib segment

Ridge

Continuous glazing

Solid podium

Ribbon window

HARBOR FACADE

Vault roof constructed of chevron-shaped precast tiles

Vault over restaurant

Staircase

Solid podium

Pink cladding

Pink granite-aggregate paving slab

Main line of support

Awning

Staircase

Terrace

WEST SIDE

57

Architectural styles

BUILDINGS CAN BE CLASSIFIED according to which of the various architectural styles they exemplify. There are three main criteria used to define a building's style: design, proportions, and ornamentation. These criteria may be influenced by various factors, including the function of a building, the materials and building techniques available, and the interests of a building's patron. The chart below shows the major architectural styles throughout the ages and across the world, with illustrations of important buildings of each style. From the chart it is possible to identify certain recurring trends, such as the importance of continuity in Far Eastern and Indian buildings, the innovative character of European architecture since medieval times, the enduring use of classical motifs, and the worldwide influence of Islamic themes.

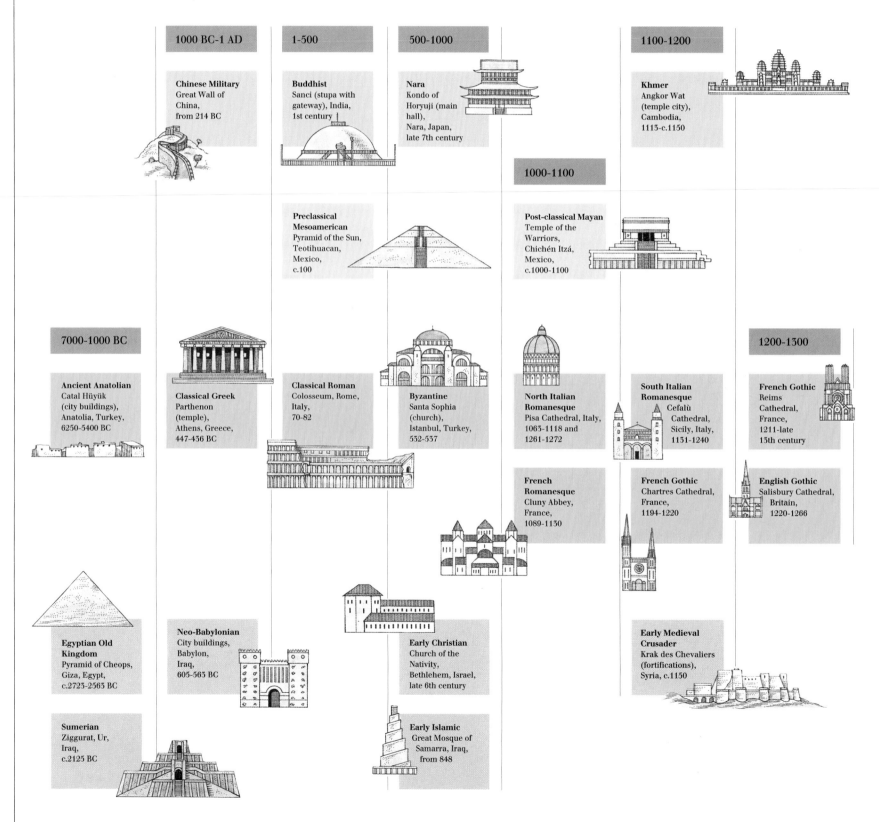

1000 BC-1 AD

Chinese Military
Great Wall of China,
from 214 BC

1-500

Buddhist
Sanci (stupa with gateway), India,
1st century

500-1000

Nara
Kondo of Horyuji (main hall),
Nara, Japan,
late 7th century

1100-1200

Khmer
Angkor Wat (temple city),
Cambodia,
1113-c.1150

1000-1100

Preclassical Mesoamerican
Pyramid of the Sun,
Teotihuacan,
Mexico,
c.100

Post-classical Mayan
Temple of the Warriors,
Chichén Itzá,
Mexico,
c.1000-1100

7000-1000 BC

Ancient Anatolian
Catal Hüyük (city buildings),
Anatolia, Turkey,
6250-5400 BC

Classical Greek
Parthenon (temple),
Athens, Greece,
447-436 BC

Classical Roman
Colosseum, Rome,
Italy,
70-82

Byzantine
Santa Sophia (church),
Istanbul, Turkey,
532-537

North Italian Romanesque
Pisa Cathedral, Italy,
1063-1118 and
1261-1272

South Italian Romanesque
Cefalù Cathedral,
Sicily, Italy,
1131-1240

1200-1300

French Gothic
Reims Cathedral,
France,
1211-late
13th century

French Romanesque
Cluny Abbey,
France,
1089-1130

French Gothic
Chartres Cathedral,
France,
1194-1220

English Gothic
Salisbury Cathedral,
Britain,
1220-1266

Egyptian Old Kingdom
Pyramid of Cheops,
Giza, Egypt,
c.2723-2563 BC

Neo-Babylonian
City buildings,
Babylon,
Iraq,
605-563 BC

Early Christian
Church of the Nativity,
Bethlehem, Israel,
late 6th century

Early Medieval Crusader
Krak des Chevaliers (fortifications),
Syria, c.1150

Sumerian
Ziggurat, Ur,
Iraq,
c.2125 BC

Early Islamic
Great Mosque of Samarra, Iraq,
from 848

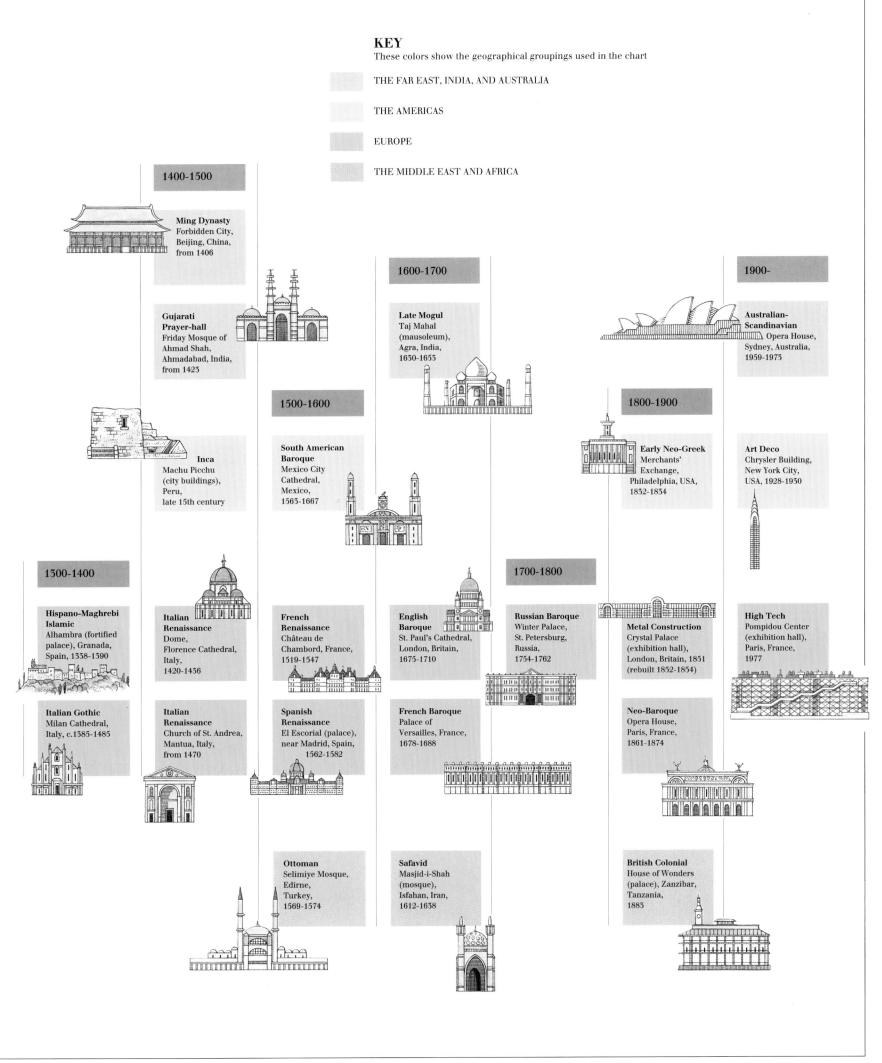

KEY
These colors show the geographical groupings used in the chart

THE FAR EAST, INDIA, AND AUSTRALIA

THE AMERICAS

EUROPE

THE MIDDLE EAST AND AFRICA

1400-1500

Ming Dynasty
Forbidden City,
Beijing, China,
from 1406

**Gujarati
Prayer-hall**
Friday Mosque of
Ahmad Shah,
Ahmadabad, India,
from 1423

1600-1700

Late Mogul
Taj Mahal
(mausoleum),
Agra, India,
1630-1653

1900-

**Australian-
Scandinavian**
Opera House,
Sydney, Australia,
1959-1973

1500-1600

Inca
Machu Picchu
(city buildings),
Peru,
late 15th century

**South American
Baroque**
Mexico City
Cathedral,
Mexico,
1563-1667

1800-1900

Early Neo-Greek
Merchants'
Exchange,
Philadelphia, USA,
1832-1834

Art Deco
Chrysler Building,
New York City,
USA, 1928-1930

1300-1400

1700-1800

**Hispano-Maghrebi
Islamic**
Alhambra (fortified
palace), Granada,
Spain, 1338-1390

**Italian
Renaissance**
Dome,
Florence Cathedral,
Italy,
1420-1436

**French
Renaissance**
Château de
Chambord, France,
1519-1547

**English
Baroque**
St. Paul's Cathedral,
London, Britain,
1675-1710

Russian Baroque
Winter Palace,
St. Petersburg,
Russia,
1754-1762

Metal Construction
Crystal Palace
(exhibition hall),
London, Britain, 1851
(rebuilt 1852-1854)

High Tech
Pompidou Center
(exhibition hall),
Paris, France,
1977

Italian Gothic
Milan Cathedral,
Italy, c.1385-1485

**Italian
Renaissance**
Church of St. Andrea,
Mantua, Italy,
from 1470

**Spanish
Renaissance**
El Escorial (palace),
near Madrid, Spain,
1562-1582

French Baroque
Palace of
Versailles, France,
1678-1688

Neo-Baroque
Opera House,
Paris, France,
1861-1874

Ottoman
Selimiye Mosque,
Edirne,
Turkey,
1569-1574

Safavid
Masjid-i-Shah
(mosque),
Isfahan, Iran,
1612-1638

British Colonial
House of Wonders
(palace), Zanzibar,
Tanzania,
1883

Index

A

Abacus
  Ancient Egyptian temple 7
  Ancient Greek building 8
  Medieval church 21
  Neoclassical building 35
Abbey of St. Foi, Conques, France 20
Abutment 38-39
Abutment pier 15
Acanthus leaf 8
Acropolis, Athens, Greece 8
Acroterion 8-9
Aedicule
  Ancient Roman building 11
  Renaissance building 26, 28
AEG Turbine Hall, Berlin, Germany 53
Air conditioning 54-55
Air duct 15
Aisle
  Ancient Egyptian temple 6
  Cathedral dome 38
  Gothic church 22, 24-25
  Medieval church 20-21
Alhambra, Granada, Spain 42, 59
Altar 22
Ambulatory corridor 13
Amphitheater 12
Anchor joint 50
Ancient Anatolian style 58
Ancient Egyptian buildings 6-7
Ancient Greek buildings 8-9, 10
Ancient Roman buildings 10-13, 26
  Tile 17
  Window 48
Angkor Wat, Cambodia 58
Angle buttress 23, 24
Anglo-Saxon style 47, 49
Angoulême Cathedral, France 20-21
Angular cincture 16
Annulet 8
Anta 9
Antarala 44-45
Antefixa 9
Apse 13, 21, 33
Arabesque
  Ceiling panel 36-37
  Neoclassical molding 32
  Islamic building 42-43
Arcade
  Ancient Roman building 12-13
  Baroque church 31-33
  Gothic building 22-23
  Medieval church 20-21
  Twentieth-century building 53
Arched brace 25
Arched doorway 47
Arched facade 51
Arches 14, 38-39
  Ancient Roman building 10, 12-13
  Asian building 44-45
  Baroque church 31, 32
  Cathedral dome 41
  Cathedral pier 15
  Door 46
  French temple 39
  Gothic church 22, 24-25
  Islamic building 42-43
  Medieval building 18-21
  Nineteenth-century building 50-51
  Renaissance building 26-27
Architectural styles 58-59
Architrave
  Ancient Egyptian temple 6-7
  Ancient Greek temple 9
  Ancient Roman building 11, 13
  Baroque church 31-33
  French temple 39

  Gothic building 25
  Neoclassical building 30, 34-35
  Renaissance building 28-29
Archivolt
  Baroque church 31, 33
  French temple 39
  Gothic church 23
  Medieval building 19, 20
  Renaissance building 29
Arch of Titus, Italy 11
Arch-plate 51
Archway 51
Arris 14
  Medieval church 21
  Molding 14
Art deco style 53, 59
  Doorway 47
  Twentieth-century building 52
Art nouveau style 53
  Doorway 47
Ashlar 12, 16, 40
Asian buildings 44-45
Asphalt 16
Astragal 40
Atlas 34
Atrium 56
Attached column
  Ancient Roman building 13
  Baroque church 32
  Gothic building 25
  Medieval building 20-21
  Neoclassical building 31
Attic
  Baroque church 32-33
  Cathedral dome 41
  Neoclassical building 30, 35
Auda 45
Auditorium 31
Aureole 23
Australian-Scandinavian style 59
Awning 57
Axle-pulley 49

B

Bage, C. 50
Bagneux Church, France 20-21
Bailey 18
Balcony 51
  Islamic tomb 43
  Nineteenth-century building 51
  Renaissance theater 29
  Rococo style 30, 34
Ballflowers 22-23
Baluster
  Asian building 44
  Gothic building 25
  Neoclassical building 35
Balustrade
  Asian building 44
  Baroque church 31-32
  Cathedral dome 41
  Gothic church 24-25
  Neoclassical building 30, 35
  Nineteenth-century building 51
  Renaissance theater 29
  Twentieth-century building 53
Bank of England, London, Britain 34
Banqueting House, Whitehall Palace, London, Britain 36-37
Barge-board 14
Baroque style 30-35, 59
  Window 49
Barrel vault 38-39
  Ancient Roman building 11-12
  Baroque church 31
  Cathedral pier 15
  Medieval church 20

Nineteenth-century building 51
Barry, C. 51
Bascule 51
Base
  Ancient Greek temple 9
  Ancient Roman building 11, 13
  Asian building 45
  Baroque church 31, 33
  Cathedral pier 15
  Dome 38, 40, 41
  French temple 39
  Gothic church 22, 24
  Medieval church 21
  Neoclassical building 30, 35
  Renaissance theater 29
  Twentieth-century building 52
Basement 35
Baseplate 40
Basilican system 20
Basilica of St. Madeleine, Vezelay, France 20
Basket arch 24, 38
Bas-relief carving 45
Bastille, Paris, France 18
Batten 47
Battlemented building 19
Battlemented cornice 23
Battlements 18
Bauhaus Building, Dessau, Germany 49
Bauhaus window 49
Bay leaf garland 32
Bay window 29
Bead 46
Bead molding 7
Beam
  Crown post 16
  Gothic church 25
  High-tension 54
  Modern building 55, 56-57
  Nineteenth-century building 50
Becket Chapel, London, Britain 19
Bed joint 14
Belfry 33
Bell chamber 51
Bell-shaped dome 45
Belvedere 28
Beveled panel 47
Beverley Minster, Yorkshire, Britain 38
"Big Ben," Palace of Westminster, London, Britain 51
Binder 12, 14
Blind arch
  Asian building 45
  Cathedral dome 41
  Gothic church 22
Blind door 30
Blind tracery 51
Blind trefoil 25
Blind window 30
Block 27, 38
Block carving 22
Board-and-plaster ceiling 36
Boarding 12
Bolection molding 46-47
Bolt 48, 57
Bonded brick wall 50
Bonding 14
  English bond 14, 39
  Flemish bond 14, 17
  Stretcher bond 14, 17
Bonnet hip tile 17
Boom 56
Border 48
Boss 20, 21
Bow front 35
Bowtell molding 27
Box 29
Box sash window 49
Brace 14, 39
  Asian building 44
  Crown post roof 16
  Dome 40
  Door 46-47
  Gothic building 25
  King post roof 16
  Neoclassical building 31

Nineteenth-century building 51
Queen post roof 16
Timber-framed house 14
Bracket
  Baroque church 31
  Cathedral dome 38
  Cathedral pier 15
  Ceiling panel 36
  Gothic building 25
  Islamic tomb 43
  Medieval building 18
  Neoclassical building 30
  Renaissance building 27
  Timber-framed house 14
  Victorian chimney 17
Breakfast room 35
Breastsummer 14
Bressumer 14
Bricklaying 14
Brick pier 53
Brick vault 50
Brick wall 14, 50
Bridges
  London Bridge 18-19
  Medieval castle 19
  Modern building 56
British colonial style 59
Broken pediment 33
Buddhist style 44, 58
Burmese pagoda 44
Butt hinge 47
Buttress 38
  Baroque church 30-33
  Cathedral pier 15
  Dome 40
  Gothic church 22-25
  Medieval building 18, 20-21
  Nineteenth-century building 51
Byzantine style 49, 58

C

Caernarvon Castle, Britain 18
Came 48
Campaniform capital 6
Campanile 29
Candelabrum 28
Canopy 24
Cantilever beams 52
Cantilevered shade 53
Capital
  Ancient Egyptian building 6-7
  Ancient Greek building 8-9
  Ancient Roman building 11, 13
  Asian building 45
  Baroque church 33
  Cathedral dome 41
  Cathedral pier 15
  Domed roof 40
  French temple 39
  Islamic mosque 42
  Medieval building 19-21
  Neoclassical building 30, 35
  Ptolemaic-Roman period 7
  Renaissance building 28-29
  Romanesque style 20
Cartouche 6
Carved stone 42
Carving 14
  Asian building 44-45
  Gothic building 22
Casa de las Conchas, Salamanca, Spain 28
Casa del Fascio, Como, Italy 53
Casement window 48
Cast iron 50-51
Castles, medieval 18-19
Cast steel 55
Çatal Hüyük, Anatolia, Turkey 58
Cathedral of St. Lazare, Autun, France 20

Cauliculus 8
Cavetto molding
  Baroque church 31
  Ancient Egyptian building 6-7
  French temple 39
  Gothic building 24
  Renaissance building 29
  Timber-framed house 14
Cavity wall 14
Cefalù Cathedral, Sicily, Italy 58
Ceilings 36-37, 38
  Ancient Roman building 11
  Panels 36-37
Cell 21, 39
Cella 9, 11, 39
Cement-rendered wall 52
Censer 42
Centre Georges Pompidou, Paris, France 54-55
Chain motif 45
Chaitya 43
Chamber 13, 45
Chamfered corner 39
Channel 8
Chapel
  Baroque church 31
  Gothic church 22
  Medieval church 21
Chapel pier 19
Chapter house 24
Chartres Cathedral, France 58
Chataya arch 45
Château de Blois, France 28
Château de Chambord, France 28, 59
Château de Montal, Lot, France 26, 28-29
Chattra 45
Chattravali 44-45
Chemise 18-19
Cherub 24, 36-37
Chevet 21
Chichén Itzá, Mexico 58
Chimneys 16-17
Chimney shaft 19
Chimney stack 17, 28, 35
Chinese military style 58
Choir
  Gothic church 22, 24
  Medieval church 20-21
Choir-aisle 25
Choir-screen 22
Choir-stall 22
Christian architecture 20
Chrysler Building, New York, USA 47, 53, 59
Church of St. Andrea, Mantua, Italy 59
Church of St. Botolph, Norfolk, Britain 25
Church of St. Eustache, Paris, France 29
Church of St. George in the East, London, Britain 30, 33
Church of St. Maclou, Rouen, France 22, 24
Church of St. Maria della Salute, Venice, Italy 30
Church of St. Maria della Vittoria, Rome, Italy 30
Church of St. Paul-St. Louis, Paris, France 30-31
Church of St. Pierre de Libreville, Gabon 54, 57
Church of St. Serge, Angers, France 21
Church of St. Zaccaria, Venice, Italy 47
Church of Santa Sophia, Turkey 41, 58
Church of the Nativity, Bethlehem, Israel 58
Church of the Sorbonne, Paris, France 40
Church roof boss 20
Cincture 16, 29
Cinquefoil molding 23
Circle 31
Cirque Napoleon, Paris, France 30-31

Cladding
  Modern building 54, 56-57
  Tiled roof 17
  Twentieth-century building 52
Cladding-panel 54
Classical Greek style 58
Classical Roman style 58
Classical-style architecture 26, 34
Clay daub 13, 14
Clay tile 16-17
Clerestory
  Ancient Egyptian temple 7
  Baroque church 31
  Cathedral pier 15
  Gothic church 24
Clock tower 51
Cloister 24
Closer 14
Cluny Abbey, France 58
Clustered column 21
Coat of arms 48
Cockpit 56
Cockspur-pattern handle 48
Coffer 11, 39
Coffered arch 15
Coffered vault 39
Coffering 27
Collar 25
Collar beam 14, 16, 25
Collar purlin 14, 16
Cologne Cathedral, Germany 46-47
Colonette
  Gothic church 25
  Islamic building 42
  Medieval building 19-21
  Neoclassical building 31
  Renaissance building 26
Colonnade
  Ancient Greek building 8-9
  Ancient Roman building 10-11
  Cathedral dome 38, 41
  Neoclassical building 35
Colonnaded story 52
Colosseum, Rome, Italy 10, 12-13, 58
Column 14
  Ancient Egyptian building 6-7
  Ancient Greek building 6, 8
  Ancient Roman building 10-11, 13
  Baroque church 32-33
  Cathedral dome 41
  French temple 39
  Gothic church 25
  Islamic mosque 42
  Medieval church 20-21
  Modern building 54-56
  Neoclassical building 30-31, 35
  Nineteenth-century building 50-51
  Renaissance building 29
Common rafter
  Crown post roof 16
  Dome 40
  Gothic building 25
  Tiled roof 17
  Timber-framed house 14
Compass 39
Composite capital 15
Composite column 30
Composite pilaster 15
Compound pier 20-21
Concave brace 14
Concave molding 34
Concave wall 30, 33
Concrete 52
Concrete floor 50, 56
Concrete frame 54
Concrete rib 57
Concrete shoe 57
Concrete wall 11, 13, 54
Conical dome 28
Conical spire 18, 28
Contant d'Ivry, P. 30
Convex portico 35
Cooling tower 54-55
Coping stone 53

Copper tingle 17
Corbel
  Cathedral dome 41
  Medieval building 19, 21
  Neoclassical building 34
  Nineteenth-century
    building 51
  Renaissance building 29
  Rococo style 30
Corinthian capital 8
  Ancient Roman
    building 11
  Baroque church 31, 33
  Cathedral pier 15
  Corinthian column 11,
    31-32
Corinthian entablature 11
Corinthian half-column 12
Corinthian order 8, 10
Corinthian pilaster
  Ancient Roman
    building 11-12
  Baroque church 32-33
Corner post 14
Cornice
  Ancient Egyptian
    temple 6-7
  Ancient Greek
    building 8-9
  Ancient Roman
    building 10-13
  Asian building 45
  Baroque church 31-33
  Cathedral pier 15
  Dome 38, 40
  French temple 39
  Gothic church 22-25
  Islamic tomb 43
  Medieval building
    18-19, 21
  Neoclassical building
    30-31, 34-35
  Nineteenth-century
    building 51
  Renaissance building
    26-29
  Twentieth-century
    building 52
Cornucopia 32, 37
Corona 27
Corridor 13, 15
Coucy-le-Château, Aisne,
  France 18-19
Counterweight 56
Couronnement 24
Course
  Asian building 45
  Brick 14
  Medieval building 18-19
  Neoclassical building 35
  Nineteenth-century
    building 50-51
  Victorian chimney 17
Courtyard 13, 18
Coussinet 8
Coved dome 30, 39
Crane 56
Crenel 18
Crenellations 18
Crepidoma 9, 33
Crest 31, 42, 51
Crocket 23-24
Cronaca 26
Cross
  Baroque church 32
  Dome 40-41
  Motif 24
Cross-bracing 55-57
Crossing 21-22
Crossing tower 20
Crown 17, 38
Crowning cornice
  Ancient Roman
    building 13
  Baroque church 31
  Renaissance building
    26-27
Crown post 14, 16
Crown post roof 16
Cruciform column 50
Cruciform pedestal 33, 41
Cruck frame 18
Crypt 15, 19
Crypt window 33
Crystal Palace Exhibition
  Hall, London, Britain
  50-51, 59
Cuneus 13
Cupola
  Baroque church 31
  Medieval building 18
  Nineteenth-century
    building 51

Curtain 29, 55
Curtain wall 18, 54, 56
Curved buttress 30-33
Curved cornice 10
Curvilinear tracery 22, 24
Cushion 8
Cusp
  Asian building 42
  Gothic building 24-25
  Timber-framed house 14
Cusped arch 43
Cyma recta 27
Cyma reversa 8, 24
Cymatium 27

D

Dado
  Baroque church 33
  French temple 39
  Neoclassical building 31
  Renaissance building 28
Dagger 24
Dagoba stupa 44-45
Da Maiano, B. 26
Dancette-pattern mosaic 43
Da Sangallo, G. 26
Daub 14
Decorated cement frieze 53
Dentil
  Ancient Roman
    building 10
  Baroque church 31, 33
  Cathedral dome 41
  French temple 39
  Neoclassical building 30
  Renaissance building 27
  Tiled roof 17
Depressed arch
  Ancient Roman
    building 10
  Islamic building 42-43
  Timber-framed house 14
Deutscher Werkbund
  style 53
Dial 51
Diaper work 48
Dog-leg staircase 33
Domed roof 43
Domed turret 51
Dome metaling 40
Dome of the Rock,
  Jerusalem, Israel 41
Domes 38, 40-41
  Ancient Roman
    building 10
  Asian building 44-45
  Baroque church 32-33
  Cathedral pier 15
  French temple 39
  Islamic building 42
  Medieval building 19, 21
  Neoclassical building 30
  Renaissance building
    27-29, 59
Dome timbering 40
Donjon 18-19
Doorbell 47
Door jamb 30
Doorknob 47
Door knocker 47
Door rail 46
Doors 46-47
  Ancient Egyptian
    tomb 6-7
  Ancient Roman
    building 11
  Baroque church 31
  Neoclassical building 30
  Renaissance theater 29
  Timber-framed house 14
Doorway 47
  Baroque church 31, 33
  Renaissance building
    26-27
  Twentieth-century
    building 53
Doric capital 8
Doric column 8
Doric half-column 12
Doric order 8
Dormer head 51
Dormer window 28, 51, 53
Double-glazed unit 49
Drain pipe 50
Dravidian finial 45
Dravidian style 44
Drawbridge 51
Drawbridge windlass 19
Dressing room 29

Drip-cap 34
Drum 40
  Ancient Greek building 8
  Baroque church 33
  Cathedral dome 41
Dubika 44
Duct 55
Dutch cubist style 53

E

Early Christian building 58
Early English Perpendicular-
  style tracery 24
Early English-style window
  24
Early medieval crusader
  style 58
Early Neo-Greek style 59
Earthenware tile 42
East Asian buildings 44-45
Eating room 35
Eaves
  Ancient Greek building 9
  Ancient Roman
    building 10, 12
  Crown post roof 16
  Islamic tomb 43
  Modern building 57
  Neoclassical building 34
  Renaissance building 29
  Tiled roof 17
  Timber-framed house 14
Eaves board 44
Echinus 8
Edge-halfed scarf joint 16
Egyptian building 6-7, 46
Egyptian old kingdom
  style 58
Eighteenth-century
  building 50
  Baroque building 33
  Neoclassical building
    30, 34-35
Eighth-century building
  44-45
El-Ainyi Mosque, Cairo,
  Egypt 43
El Escorial Palace, Madrid,
  Spain 59
Elevator 55
Elevator doorway 47
Eleventh-century building
  18, 20, 49
Ellipsoid doorway 47
Ellipsoid orb 40
Empire State Building, New
  York, USA 52
Engaged column 21
Engaged pediment 10-11
Engineering 54
Engineering brick 14
English baroque style
  32-33, 59
English bond brickwork
  14, 39
English Decorated style 22
English Gothic style 58
English Perpendicular
  style 22
Entablature
  Ancient Greek
    building 8
  Ancient Roman
    building 10-13
  Baroque church 32-33
  Cathedral dome 41
  Cathedral pier 15
  French temple 39
  Neoclassical building
    30-31, 34-35
Entasis 9
Entresol 19
Entrance
  Islamic tomb 43
  Medieval building 18-19
  Modern building 54-57
  Neoclassical building 35
  Nineteenth-century
    building 51
  Twentieth-century
    building 52
Erechtheion, Athens,
  Greece 47
Escalator 55-56
Escutcheon 47
Euthynteria 8
Expressionist style 53
Extrados 38-39, 48

F

Facade
  Ancient Greek building 9
  Ancient Roman
    building 13
  Baroque church 32-33
  Gothic church 22-24
  Modern building 54-57
  Neoclassical building
    30, 35
  Nineteenth-century
    building 51
  Renaissance building 26
Facade pediment 33
Facade wall 22
Face 14
False door 6-7
Fanlight 48
Fan vault 38-39
Far Eastern buildings 58
Fascia
  Ancient Roman building
    11-12
  Baroque church 31, 33
  Dome 40
  Domed roof 40
  French temple 39
  Gothic building 24
  Medieval building 19, 21
  Modern building 56
  Neoclassical building 34
  Renaissance building
    28-29
Fenestration 26, 52
Festoon
  Ancient Roman building
    10-11
  Cathedral dome 41
  Cathedral pier 15
  Neoclassical building
    30-31
Fifteenth century
  Mihrab 42
  Renaissance building
    26-27
  Style 10, 22, 59
  Terraces 44
  Timber-framed house 14
  Tracery 24
Fillet
  Ancient Greek temple 9
  Ceiling panel 37
  Dome 40
  French temple 39
  Gothic building 22
  Neoclassical molding 32
  Renaissance building
    27, 29
Finial
  Asian building 44-45
  Baroque church 31, 33
  Gothic church 22-23
  Islamic building 42-43
  Medieval building 20
  Neoclassical building 30
  Nineteenth-century
    building 51
  Renaissance building 28
  Roof 16
Fire escape 55-56
Fireplace 16, 18-19
Fire-resistant curtain 55
Fire-resistant panel 54
First century
  Building 10-12
  Style 58
Fish-scale tile 28-29, 40
Flagpole 53
Flamboyant tracery 24
Flange 50, 56
Flat roof 16
  Ancient Egyptian
    building 6
  Neoclassical building 35
  Twentieth-century
    building 52-53
Flat soffit 12
Flavian amphitheater,
  Italy 12
Flax-spinning mill,
  Shrewsbury, Britain 50
Flemish bond 14, 17
Flint facing brick 14
Floor 36
  Cathedral pier 15
  Modern building 54-56
  Nineteenth-century
    building 50
  Twentieth-century
    building 52-53
Floorboard 12, 14, 40

Floor joist 12, 14
Florence Cathedral, Italy
  27, 41, 59
Flue 16
Flush window 52
Fluted pilaster 10
Fluted pinnacle 33
Fluted shaft 30
Fluting 9, 11
Flying buttress
  Gothic building 22-25
  Medieval building
    18, 20-21
  Nineteenth-century
    building 51
Foliated capital 21
Foliated frieze 31
Foliated panel 31
Foliated scrollwork 24
Foliated volute 28
Footbridge 51
Forbidden City, Beijing,
  China 59
Formeret 21, 31
Fortifications 18, 58
Fortified palace 59
Forum of Trajan, Rome,
  Italy 11
Foster, N. 54, 56
Foundation
  Ancient Roman
    building 12
  Cathedral pier 15
  Modern building 54
  Nineteenth-century
    building 50
Four-paneled door 47
Fourteenth century 26
  Arch 42
  Gothic building 23-25
  Medieval building 18-19
  Roof 44
  Style 22
Frame
  Door 46-47
  Medieval house 18
  Modern building 54
  Roof 16
  Steel 52
  Timber 14
  Window 48
Frame-construction walls 14
French baroque style 31,
  34, 59
French Flamboyant style 22
French Gothic style 58
French Renaissance
  style 59
French Romanesque
  style 58
Fret-pattern mosaic 42-43
Fretwork 9, 45
Friday Mosque of Ahmad
  Shah, Ahmadabad,
  India 59
Frieze
  Ancient Egyptian
    building 7
  Ancient Greek building 9
  Ancient Roman building
    11, 13
  Baroque church 33
  Cathedral dome 41
  Cathedral pier 15
  French temple 39
  Medieval church 21
  Neoclassical building
    30-31, 34
  Renaissance building 28
  Twentieth-century
    building 53
Frog 14
Front door 47
Functionalism 54

G

Gable
  Gothic building 22-25
  Medieval building 19, 21
  Nineteenth-century
    building 50-51
  Renaissance building 28
  Timber-frame house 14
Gable-and-valley roof 17
Gabled arch 23
Gallery
  Ancient Roman
    building 13
  Baroque church 31-32

Cathedral dome 41
Medieval building
  18-20
Modern building 54-55
Renaissance theater 29
Gambrel roof 44
Gangway 12
Gargoyle 25
Gate 44-45
Gate house 19
Gate of the Sun, Tiahuanaco,
  Bolivia 47
Gateway 8, 58
Gauged arch 50
Gentlemen's room 29
Gerberette 55
German-style baroque 34
Gilded band 44
Gilded cross 41
Gilded orb 41
Gilded rib 41
Gilt ironwork 34
Girder 51
Glass 50, 52
Glass curtain 55
Glass mosaic 43
Glass pane 48
Glass panel 46
Glass wall 54, 57
Glazed window 48
Glazing
  Modern building 54-57
  Twentieth-century
    building 52
Glazing bar 48-49, 57
Glazing bead 46, 49
Globe Theater, London,
  Britain 29
Glulam wall plate 57
Glyph 8
Gopuram finial 45
Gothic architecture 20,
  22-25, 58-59
Gothic portal 47
Gothic stone arch 19
Gothic-style door 47
Gothic torus 22
Granite-aggregate slab 57
Granite cladding 52
Great Mosque, Cordoba,
  Spain 38
Great Wall of China 58
Greek-style fret ornament 35
Griffon 9
Grille 12
Groin 39
Groin vault 31, 38-39
Grotesque figure 28
Grundtvig Church,
  Copenhagen, Denmark 53
Gruppo Seven Cubist 53
Gryphon 9
Guilloche 47
Gujarati Prayer-hall,
  Ahmadabad, India 59
Gutter 40, 50

H

Half-column 12, 20-21
Half-truss 16
Hall
  Asian building 45
  Hypostyle 6
  Medieval building 18-19
  Modern building 54, 56
  Neoclassical building 35
"Hall-keeps" 18
Hammer 39
Hammer-beam roof 22, 25
Hammer-post 25
Handle 47, 49
Handle-plate 48
Handrail
  Modern building 56
  Renaissance building 29
  Twentieth-century
    building 52
Hanger 56
Harmika 45
Harmon, A.L. 52
Haunch 38
Hawksmoor, N. 30, 33
Head 48
Headers
  Brickwork 14, 39
  Nineteenth-century
    building 50
  Tiled roof 17
Helicopter landing-pad 56

Hemispherical dome 29, 40-41
Herringbone pattern 42
Hieroglyphs 6-7
High altar 22
High tech style 59
High-tension beam 54
Himeji Castle, Himeji, Japan 44
Hinge 48
Hip 53
Hipped roof 16-17, 28-29
Hip rafter 16-17, 44
Hispano-Maghrebi Islamic style 59
Historiated boss 21
Historiated keystone 21
Hittorff, J.I. 31
Hollow roll joint 17
Hong Kong and Shanghai Bank, Hong Kong 54, 56
Hood mold 33, 40
Hoover Factory, London, Britain 53
Horn 48
Horseshoe arch 38
Horsley Church, Derbyshire, Britain 25
Hotel des Invalides, Paris, France 49
House
    Door 47
    Medieval **18-19**
    Timber-frame 14
House of Wonders, Zanzibar, Tanzania 59
Hti 44
Hypostyle hall 6
Hypaethral temple 8

I

Impost
    Ancient Roman building 13
    Cathedral dome 38
    Gothic building 25
    Islamic building 42
    Medieval building 18, 21
Inca building 59
Incline 20
Industrial Revolution 50
Inlay 42-43
Inner dome 15
Inscription 42
Intercolumniation 9, 39
Intrados 21, 38, 48
Inverted ovolo 40
Ionic capital 8
    Baroque church 33
    French temple 39
    Renaissance building 28
Ionic column
    Baroque church 33
    French temple 39
    Neoclassical building 35
Ionic doorway 47
Ionic half-column 12
Ionic order 8
Iron 50
Iron railing 51
Iron roof 31
Iron shaft 48
Iron tracery 51
Ironwork 30
Ish Khan Church, Tortum, Turkey 49
Islamic buildings **42-43**, 58-59
Islamic mosaic 43
Italian Gothic style 59
Italian Renaissance style 59

J

Jacket wall 18
Jack-rafter 16-17, 25
Jali 42-43
Jamb
    Ancient Roman temple 11
    Baroque church 31
    Medieval church 20
    Neoclassical building 30, 34-35
    Nineteenth-century building 50

Jami Masjid, Bijapur, India 42
Jettied joist 14
Jetty plate 14
Joist 12, 14, 40
Jones, H. 51
Jones, I. 36

K

Kalasa finial 43
Kasugado Shrine of Enjoji, Nara, Japan 44
Kasuga-style roof 44
Kawana House, Japan 54
Keeled lesene 40
Keep 18
Kerb principal rafter 16
Keyhole escutcheon 47
Keystone 38
    Ancient Roman building 11, 13
    Baroque church 31, 33
    French temple 39
    Medieval church 21
    Neoclassical building 30, 34
    Renaissance building 28-29
King post 25, 31
King post roof truss 16
King strut 12
Knocker 47
Kondo of Horyuji, Nara, Japan 58

L

Label mold 33
Lady Chapel, Salisbury Cathedral, Britain 22
Lamb-hinge 47
Lamb, T. 52
Lancet 23
Lancet arch 25, 38
Lancet window 14, 22-24
Landing 29
Lantern 40
    Baroque church 32-33
    French temple 39
    Neoclassical building 30-31
    Twentieth-century building 52
Latch 47-48
Late Mogul style 59
Lath 12, 14, 17
Lattice beam 54-55
Latticed screen 42-43
Latticed shade 53
Lattice truss 57
Lattice window 50
Latticework 51
Laurentian Library, Florence, Italy 26-27
Lead came 48
Lead covering 41
Lead roof 16-17
Lean-to roof 20-22, 24
Le Corbusier 52
Lemercier, J. 40
Lesbian leaf pattern 8
Lesene
    Ancient Roman building 10
    Baroque church 32-33
    Dome 40
    French temple 39
    Gothic church 25
    Renaissance building 28-29
Library 35, 54
Lierne 21
Light
    Renaissance building 26
    Twentieth-century building 53
    Window 48
Light well 41
Limestone block 22
Limestone cladding 52
Limestone false door 7
Lintel 7, 52
Lintel course 35
Load-bearing wall 14
Lobby 56
Lock 47

Lock rail 47
Loft 29
London Bridge, Britain 18-19
Loophole
    Medieval building 18-21
    Renaissance building 29
Lotus flower 42
Lotus petal 43
Louver 51, 56
Lozenge 23, 39
Lucarne window 32-33, 40
Lund Cathedral, Sweden 46-47
Lunette 15, 32
Lunette design 47

M

Madeleine, Paris, France 30
Maenianum summum 13
Mail slot plate 47
Main vessel 15
Mandapa 45
Mannerism 26
Mansard roof 44
Marble-filled opening 41
Marble mosaic 43
Marble veneer 10
Margin 17
Martellange, E. 31
Mascaron 41
Mask 8, 41
Masonry 14
    Ancient Roman building 13
    Cathedral dome 38
    Neoclassical building 34
Masonry apron 41
Mason's mark 22
Mason's tools 39
Mass-construction wall 14
Mass-produced brick 14
Mass-production 50
Matchboarded door 46-47
Mausoleum 59
Meander 9
Medallion 28
Medieval castles **18-19**
Medieval churches **20-21**
Medieval crusader style 58
Medieval houses 14, **18-19**
Medieval wall ornament 14
Medinet Habu, Egypt 7
Merchants' Exchange, Philadelphia, USA 51, 59
Merlon 18
Metal construction style 59
Metal-frame wall 14
Metal-frame window 48
Metaling 40
Metal panel 54-55
Metope 8
Metric brick 14
Mexico City Cathedral, Mexico 59
Mezzanine 19, 54
Mihrab 42
Milan Cathedral, Italy 25, 59
Mill 10, 12, 50
Minaret 42-43
Ming Dynasty style 59
Moat 18-19
Modern buildings **54-57**
Modillion
    Baroque church 31
    Ceiling panel 36
    Neoclassical building 30
    Renaissance building 27
Mogul style 59
Molded bracket 15, 38
Molded corbel 51
Molded stucco 36-37
Molding 39
    Ancient Egyptian temple 6-7
    Asian building 44
    Baroque church 32-33
    Dome 40-41
    Door 46-47
    Gothic church 23-24
    Medieval building 18, 21
    Neoclassical building 31-32, 34
    Renaissance building 27, 29
    Timber-framed house 14
    Victorian chimney 17
    Window 48

Monolithic shaft 11
Monument 22
Moorish arch 38
Mortar 17
Mortise 46
Mortise and tenon joint 16
    Dome 40
    Door 46
    Nineteenth-century building 50
Mosaic 42-43
Mosque 42
Mosque, Ahmadabad, India 59
Mother-of-pearl mosaic 43
Motte 18
Mouchette 24
Mud daub 14
Mullion 48
    Cathedral pier 15
    Gothic church 22, 24-25
    Modern building 55-57
    Renaissance building 28
    Twentieth-century building 52
Multifoil 15
Multi-gabled roof 50
Muntin 46-47, 49
Music gallery 29

N

Naos
    Ancient Greek building 9
    Ancient Roman building 11
    French temple 39
Nave
    Ancient Egyptian temple 6-7
    Baroque church 31
    Cathedral dome 38
    Gothic church 22-25
    Medieval church 20-21
Neo-Babylonian style 58
Neo-Baroque style 50-51, 59
Neo-Byzantine style 50-51
Neoclassical style **50-35**, 54
Neo-Gothic style 50
Neo-Greek style 50-51, 59
New State Paper Office, London, Britain 34
Niche
    Ancient Roman building 10
    Asian temple 45
    Baroque church 32
    Cathedral dome 41
    Cathedral pier 15
    Gothic church 23-24
    Islamic building 42
    Medieval building 19
    Neoclassical building 34
    Renaissance building 28
Nineteenth-century buildings 31, 34, **50-51**, 52
Ninth-century building 44
Node 55
Nonesuch House, London Bridge, Britain 19
North Italian Romanesque style 58
Notre Dame de Paris, France 22, 25

O

Oak sill 48
Octafoil 23
Octahedral column 51
Octahedral dome 33
Octahedral shaft 51
Octahedral turret 51
Octastyle portico 10
Oculus
    Ancient Roman building 10-11
    Gothic church 24-25
    Medieval building 18, 21
    Neoclassical building 35
Oeil-de-boeuf window 48-49
    Baroque church 31, 33
    Cathedral dome 41
Ogee arch 42
Ogee-arched motif 44
Ogee brace 51
Ogee curve 24

Monolithic shaft 11
Monument 22
Moorish arch 38
Mortar 17

Ogee-curved dome 40
Ogee-curved roof 40
Ogee molding 27-29, 33
Ogee tracery 51
Onion dome 19, 40-42
Opera House, Paris, France 51, 59
Opera House, Sydney, Australia 57, 59
Opisthodomos 9
Opus incertum 11, 13
Opus quadratum 13
Opus sectile mosaic 42-43
Orb 40
    Baroque church 32
    Cathedral dome 41
    Gothic church 25
    Neoclassical building 31
    Nineteenth-century building 51
    Renaissance building 29
Orchestra shell 53
Organ 22, 24
Oriel window 14, 19
Ornament
    Asian building 45
    Baroque church 31, 33
    Cathedral dome 41
    Islamic building 42
    Neoclassical building 35
    Ornamental arch plate 51
Ornamental metalwork 45
Ornamental paneling 29
Ornamental woodwork 19
Ornamentation 52, 58
Ornamented ceiling 36
Ottoman style 59
Outer dome 15
Oversailing fascia 40
Ovolo 40
Ovolo molding
    Cathedral dome 41
    Gothic church 24
    Neoclassical building 32
    Window 48
Ovum 10
"Ox-eye" window 48-49
    Baroque church 31, 33
    Cathedral dome 41

P

Padmakosa 43
Pagoda 44
Painted roof 31
Paintings 42
Palace of Versailles, France 34, 59
Palace of Westminster, London, Britain 50-51
Palais de Fontainebleau, France 28
Palatine Chapel, Aix-la-Chapelle, France 58
Palau Güell, Barcelona, Spain 47
Palazzo Stanga, Cremona, Italy 34
Palazzo Strozzi, Florence, Italy 26-27
Paling 18, 29
Palmette
    Ancient Greek building 8-9
    Neoclassical building 31-32
Pane 48-49, 52
Panel 39
    Asian building 45
    Baroque church 31-33
    Cathedral dome 41
    Ceiling 36-37
    Door 46-47
    Gothic building 25
    Islamic building 42
    Medieval building 14, 18, 21
    Modern building 55-56
    Neoclassical building 30-31
    Nineteenth-century building 51
    Renaissance building 27
    Timber-framed house 14
    Twentieth-century building 52
Paneled door 46-47
Paneling 15, 29, 51
Panel molding 46
Pantheon, Rome, Italy 10-11

Pantile 12, 34
Papyriform column 7
Paraboloid roof 54, 57
Parapet
    Ancient Roman building 13
    Asian building 45
    Baroque church 33
    Dome 40
    Gothic church 22-24
    Islamic tomb 43
    Medieval building 19
    Neoclassical building 30, 35
    Nineteenth-century building 51
    Twentieth-century building 52
Parapet rail 35
Parthenon, Athens, Greece 9, 58
Passageway
    Ancient Roman building 11, 13
    Cathedral dome 38
    Cathedral pier 15
    Medieval building 19
Passing brace 25
Patera
    Ceiling 36-37
    Neoclassical building 32
    Renaissance building 28
Pattern 17
Paved floor 50
Pavilion 43, 53
Pavilion, Nara, Japan 58
Pavilion roof 17
Paving slab 57
Paxton, J. 50-51
Pazzi Chapel, Florence, Italy 27
Pedestal
    Ancient Roman building 10
    Baroque church 32-33
    Cathedral pier 15
    Dome 38, 40-41
    French temple 39
    Neoclassical building 31
    Renaissance building 28
Pediment
    Ancient Greek building 8
    Ancient Roman building 10-11
    Baroque church 32-33
    Neo-Baroque building 51
    Neoclassical building 30
    Renaissance building 28
Pediment ornament 8
Pendentive
    Baroque church 31
    Cathedral dome 38
    Cathedral pier 15
    Islamic mosque 42
Pentroof 44
Pepper-pot lantern 33
Perforated window 44-45
Peripteral temple 8
Peristyle 9
Perpend 14
Perpendicular-style tracery 24
Petal molding 32
Piano nobile 26, 52
Piano, R. 54
Piazza 26
Pier 14-15, 38
    Ancient Egyptian temple 7
    Ancient Roman building 13
    Baroque church 32
    Gothic church 22
    Medieval building 19-21
    Renaissance building 28-29
    Twentieth-century building 52-53
Pier buttress 21-22, 40
Pietra dura inlay 43
Pilaster 14
    Ancient Greek building 9
    Ancient Roman building 11-13
    Asian temple 44-45
    Baroque church 31-33
    Cathedral dome 38, 41
    Cathedral pier 15
    Gothic church 23
    Neoclassical building 30, 35
    Renaissance building 28
Pilaster capital 35, 41
Pilaster-strip 33

Pile foundation 54
Pillar
  Asian buildings 44-45
  Domed roof 40
  Gothic church 24
  Renaissance building 29
Pilotis 52
Pin 17, 40
Pinhead 16
Pin joint 56-57
Pinnacle
  Baroque church 31, 33
  Gothic church 22, 24-25
  Medieval church 21
  Nineteenth-century
    building 51
  Renaissance building 28
Pinpoint 16
Pisa Cathedral, Pisa, Italy 58
Pitched roof 16
  Ancient Roman building
    10, 12
  Gothic church 23-24
  Medieval building 18-20
  Nineteenth-century
    building 50
  Renaissance building
    28-29
  Timber-framed house 14
  Twentieth-century
    building 53
Plain pilaster 32
Plan 9, 45
Plant capital 7
Plaster 36
  Ancient Roman building
    12-13
  Ceiling panels 37
  Timber-framed house 14
Platband 33
Plate 14, 51
Plate connector 57
Platform
  Cathedral dome 41
  Medieval building 19-20
  Modern building 56
Platform stage 29
Plat lesene 32
Plaza 56
Plinth
  Baroque church 32
  French temple 39
  Islamic tomb 43
  Modern building 57
  Neoclassical building
    31, 35
  Renaissance building 28
  Twentieth-century
    building 52-53
Podium 11, 57
Pointed arch 19, 21, 24
Polyhedral dome 40-41
Pompidou Centre Exhibition
  Hall, Paris, France 59
Popchu-Sa Temple, Popchu-
  Sa, South Korea 44
Porch 22-23
Portal 46-47
  Baroque church 32
  Renaissance building 28
Porta Nigra, Trier, Germany
  10, 13
Porthole 41
Portico
  Ancient Greek building
    8-9
  Ancient Roman building
    10-11
  Neoclassical building
    54-55
  Renaissance building 27
Post 33, 40, 48
Post-classical Mayan style 58
Postmodernism 54
Pot 16-17
Pradakshina 45
Prairie style 53
Preclassical Mesoamerican
  style 58
Principal rafter
  Ancient Roman mill 12
  Crown post roof 16
  Dome 40
  Gothic building 25
  King post roof truss 16
  Timber-framed house 14
Processional path 22
Pronaos 9
Propylaeum 8
Prostyle colonnade 55
Pseudo-Corinthian capital 28
Pteron 8-9, 11
Ptolemaic-Roman period 7

Pugin, A.W.N. 51
Pulley 49
Purlin 16, 25
Putto 28
Pyramid 6
Pyramid of Cheops, Giza,
  Egypt 58
Pyramid of the Sun,
  Teotihuacan, Mexico 58

Q

Quadrant arch 20
Quadrilateral 43
Quadripartite vault 21
Quarrel 48
Quatrefoil 23-25
Queen post 25
Queen post roof truss 16
Quoin
  Baroque church 33
  Medieval building 18
  Nineteenth-century
    building 50
  Renaissance building 28

R

Rabbet 48
Radial wall 13
Radio mast 52
Raft 54
Rafter 16
  Ancient Roman mill 12
  Dome 40
  Gothic building 25
  Modern building 57
  Nineteenth-century
    building 50
  Tiled roof 17
  Timber-framed house 14
Rail 46
  Box sash window 49
  Door 47
  Neoclassical building 35
  Timber-framed house 14
  Window 48
Railing
  Asian building 44-45
  Cathedral dome 41
  Medieval building 19
  Nineteenth-century
    building 51
  Renaissance theater 29
Rainhill Asylum, Britain 47
Raking cornice
  Ancient Greek building
    8-9
  Ancient Roman building
    10-11
  Baroque church 32-33
  Neoclassical building 30
Ramp 19, 52
Rebate 48
Recessed arch 42
Rectangular pier 13
Rectangular window
  Ancient Roman
    building 13
  Asian building 44
  Baroque church 33
  Medieval building 18
  Renaissance building
    26, 28
Re-entrant angle 39
Re-entrant corner 31
Regula 9
Reims Cathedral, France 58
Reinforced concrete 52, 55
Reinforced plinth 57
Relief 6
Relieving arch
  Ancient Roman
    building 10
  Cathedral pier 15
  Medieval building 18-19
  Renaissance buildings
    26-29, 59
Renaissance doorway 47
Reredos 22
Return 40-41, 48
Revivalist style 51-52
Rib
  Baroque church 31
  Dome 40-41
  Medieval church 21
  Modern building 57

Ribbon window 57
Rib vault 21, 38-39
  Gothic building 22
  Medieval building 19
  Renaissance building 29
Ridge
  Crown post roof 16
  Gothic building 25
  King post roof
    truss 16
  Modern building 57
  Nineteenth-century
    building 50
  Timber-framed house 14
  Twentieth-century
    building 53
Ridge and furrow glass
  roof-window 51
Ridge and furrow roof 50
Ridge board 25
Ridge rib 21, 39
Ridge tile 12, 28
Ripley Church School, Britain
  47
Riser 29
Robie House, Chicago, USA
  53
Rocker-beam 54-55
Rococo style 30
Rogers, R. 54
Roller blind 55
Roll joint 17
Roman architecture 10-13, 58
Roman Empire 6, 10
Romanesque portal 47
Romanesque style 20, 22, 58
Roman mill 12
Roman tile 17
Roof boss 20
Roofed space 31
Roofing tile 34
Roofless temple 8
Roofs 16-17, 58
  Ancient Egyptian temple
    6-7
  Ancient Roman
    building 10
  Asian building 44
  Baroque church 33
  Dome 40
  Gothic building 22-25
  Hammer-beam 22, 25
  Islamic building 42-43
  Medieval building 19-20
  Modern building 57
  Neoclassical building
    31, 35
  Nineteenth-century
    building 50
  Renaissance building
    28-29
  Twentieth-century
    building 52-53
Roof truss 16, 25
Rope and paterae
  decoration 7
Rope and paterae
  decoration 7
Rosette
  Ceiling 36-37
  Neoclassical building 32
  Window 48
Rotunda 10-11, 34
Round arch
  Ancient Roman building
    12-13
  Baroque church 31-32
  Cathedral pier 15
  Dome 38, 40-41
  Door 46
  French temple 39
  Gothic church 25
  Medieval building 19-21
  Nineteenth-century
    building 51
  Renaissance building
    26-27
Round-arched hollow 15
Round-arched window
  Ancient Roman
    building 13
  Baroque church 33
  Dome 40
  Medieval building 18,
    20-21
  Neoclassical building 30
Royal Courts of Justice,
  London, Britain 48
Rubens, P.P. 36
Russian baroque style 59
Rustication
  Neoclassical building 31,
    34-35
  Renaissance building
    26-27

S

Sacristy 22
Saddle bar 48
St. Basil's Cathedral,
  Russia 41
St. Paul's Cathedral, London,
  Britain 59
  Arch 38
  Baroque style 30, 32-33
  Dome 40-41
  Old 22, 24
  Wall 14-15
Salient 18
Salisbury Cathedral, Britain
  22-23, 58
Sandstone 43
Sandstone brick 14
Sandstone tile 17
Santa Sophia Church,
  Istanbul, Turkey 58
Sash cord 48-49
Sash window 48-49
Saucer dome 40-41
  Ancient Roman
    building 10
  Cathedral pier 15
Scissor brace 25
Scotia 11, 39
Screen
  French baroque
    building 34
  Islamic building 42-43
  Twentieth-century
    building 52
Scrolled buttress 30
Scroll motif 22, 47
Scroll molding 18
Scroll ornament 28
Scroll-shaped corbel 34
Scrollwork 24
Sculptural decoration 19
Sculpture 51, 53
Seating 13
Second-century building 10
Segmental arch 15
Segmental head 48
Segmental pediment 10
Selimiye Mosque, Edirne,
  Turkey 59
Semi-arch 22-23
Semicircular barrel vault 51
Semicircular tower 13
Semidome
  Cathedral dome 38
  Cathedral pier 15
  Islamic mosque 42
  Neoclassical building 34
Semi-elliptical arch 38
Service shaft 56
Set-back buttress 33
Seventeenth century 26
  Building 31-33, 42
  Capital 44
  Cathedral pier 15
  Ceiling 36
  Dome 40-41
  Roof 44
  Style 30
  Tomb 43
  Window 48
Seventh century
  Building 45
  Style 58
Shaft
  Ancient Egyptian
    column 7
  Ancient Greek temple 9
  Ancient Roman building
    11, 13
  Asian building 44-45
  French temple 39
  Medieval church 20-21
  Modern building 56
  Neoclassical building
    30, 35
  Nineteenth-century
    building 51
  Window 48
Sheet-iron louver 51
Shell 12
Shell decoration 28
Shoe 57
Shop stall 14
Shreve, R.H. 52
Shrine 44-45
Sickle motif 45
Side aisle
  Cathedral dome 38
  Cathedral pier 15
  Gothic church 24-25
  Medieval church 21

Side chapel 21-22, 31
Side entrance 33
Sill
  Ancient Roman mill 12
  Box sash window 49
  Renaissance building 27
  Timber-framed
    house 14
  Twentieth-century
    building 52
  Window 48
Sixteenth century
  Building 28-29
  Ceiling 36
  Roof tile 17
  Staircase 24
  Style 10, 22
  Window 48
Sixth-century style 58
Skylight 51-52
Skyscraper 52
Slab
  Ancient Egyptian
    building 6-7
  Modern building 57
  Twentieth-century
    building 52
Slate 16
Slate tile 17
Sloped turret-roof 17
Sloping roof 40
Soane, J. 30, 34-35
Socket 48
Socle
  Ancient Egyptian
    temple 6
  Baroque church 31
  Cathedral dome 41
  Cathedral pier 15
  Gothic church 24
  Medieval church 21
  Neoclassical building
    30-31
  Renaissance building 26
Soffit 12, 38, 56
Solarium 52
Solar panel 54
South American baroque
  style 59
South Asian buildings 44-45
South Italian Romanesque
  style 59
Span 38
Spandrel
  Ceiling panel 37
  Gothic church 23
  Islamic building 42-43
  Neoclassical building 34
  Nineteenth-century
    building 51
  Renaissance building 26
Spanish Renaissance style 59
Spiral scroll 8
Spiral staircase 24, 28
Spire
  Asian building 44-45
  Gothic church 22-23, 25
  Medieval building 18, 20
  Nineteenth-century
    building 51
  Renaissance building
    28-29
Splayed windowsill 27, 34
Springing point 38-39
  Cathedral dome 38
  Cathedral pier 15
  Crown post 16
  Medieval building 19
Square 39
Square masonry 13
Square-paneled window 49
Square rib 40
Squinch 18
Staff 14
Staff-bead 49
Stage 29, 53
Stage-door 29
Stained glass 22, 48
Staircase
  Ancient Roman
    building 13
  Baroque church 33
  Gothic church 22, 24
  Medieval building 18
  Modern building 54-55, 57
  Neoclassical building 35
  Renaissance building
    26-27, 29
  Timber-framed house 14
Staircase door 47
Staircase turret 20
Stairs 29
Stairway 43

Standing seam joint 17
Starling 19
Statue 24, 30
Statuette 33
Stave 14
Stay 48
Steel 50
Steel and concrete floor 56
Steel-and-glass building 52
Steel brace 51
Steel Casement window 48
Steel column 55-56
Steel floor plate 55
Steel lattice-beam 55
Steel-lattice mullion 55
Steel mullion 52
Steel-reinforced concrete 52
Steel rod 16
Stela 7
Steeple 23, 33
Stepped roof 33
Steps
  Medieval building 19
  Modern building 57
  Neoclassical building 35
  Twentieth-century
    building 53
Stile
  Box sash window 49
  Door 46-47
  Window 48
Stilt 52
Stilted arch 20
Stoa 8
Stone 14
  Ancient Roman building
    11, 13
  Islamic building 42
Stone arch 19
Stone band 43
Stone block 33
Stone course 17
Stone foundation 50
Stone lintel 52
Stone panel 51
Stone plinth 53
Stone slab 6
Stone wall 33
Stone window 45
Story 51
Strap hinge 47
Stretcher
  Brickwork 14, 39
  Nineteenth-century
    building 50
  Tiled roof 17
Stretcher bond 14, 17
String course
  Ancient Roman
    building 13
  Cathedral dome 41
  Medieval building 18-19
  Nineteenth-century
    building 51
Strut
  Dome 38, 40
  Gothic building 25
  Neoclassical building 31
Stucco 36-37
Stud
  Ancient Roman mill 12
  Door 47
  Timber-framed house 14
Studio Elvira, Munich,
  Germany 53
Study 29
Stupa 44-45
Stupa, Sanci, India 58
Stupica 45
Stylobate 8
Sumigi 44
Sun scoop 56
Sun-shade louver 56

T

Tabernacle
  Ancient Roman
    building 11
  Renaissance building
    26, 28
Tablet flower 42, 45
Tack 17
Taenia 8
Taj Mahal, Agra, India 59
Tas-de-charge 21
Temple 38-39
  Ancient Egyptian 6
  Ancient Greek 8-9, 58
  Ancient Roman 10-11